JEBB A. HARRIS, COURIER-JOURNAL AND LOUISVILLE TIMES

The 36th Annual Pictures of the Year Competition, upon which this book is based, is supported by an educational grant from Nikon, Inc.

the best of PHOTOJOURNALISM 4

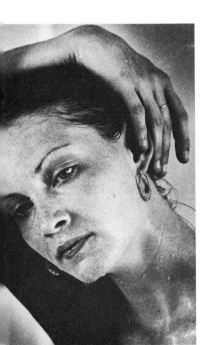

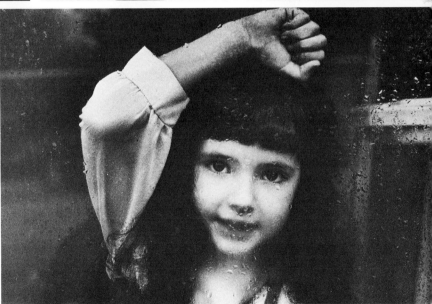

NEWSWEEK BOOKS, New York

National Press Photographers Association
University of Missouri School of Journalism

Title page, top row (left to right): GEORGE
WEDDING, PALM BEACH POST-TIMES, DAN
WHITE, THE MUSKEGON CHRONICLE,
RICARDO J. FERRO, ST. PETERSBURG TIMES
EVENING INDEPENDENT (THIRD PLACE,
FEATURE PICTURE STORY); MELISSA FAR-
LOW, COURIER-JOURNAL AND LOUISVILLE
TIMES; DAVID PETERSON, DES MOINES
REGISTER. Bottom row (left to right):
TOM KASSER, SAN BERNARDINO SUN; DAN
WHITE, THE MUSKEGON CHRONICLE;
RAYMOND K. GEHMAN, COLUMBIA MIS-
SOURIAN; PETER MONSEES, THE (HACKEN-
SACK, N.J.) RECORD.

Published in cooperation with the National Press Photographers Association,
Ken Cooke, Chairman, Book Committee.

Editorial matter, other textual material
and compilation © 1979 by the National
Press Photographers Association Foun-
dation, Inc., Seattle, Washington.

For information concerning the Pictures
of the Year Competition contact Charles
Cooper, Executive Secretary of the National Press Photographers Association,
Box 1146, Durham, North Carolina
27702.

Library of Congress Card
Number 77-081586
ISBN 0-88225-275-5

CONTENTS

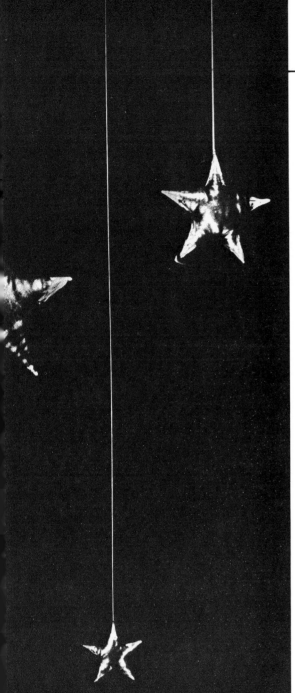

NICK KELSH, COLUMBIA (MISSOURI) DAILY TRIBUNE

Edwin D. Bayrd, Jr. Editorial Director
Mary Ann Joulwan Art Director
Ava Swarz Contributing Editor
Danielle Woerner-Bobrick Assistant Editor

Alvin Garfin Publisher

EVERY SCHOOLCHILD knows the familiar adage "A picture is worth a thousand words." It is only adults, especially those who have grown up to be newspaper and magazine editors, who seem, from time to time, to have forgotten the wisdom in that old saw, especially when it comes to choosing photographs for their publications. Most editors begin their careers as reporters, not photographers, and it is therefore altogether natural that they should allow their preference for the printed word to influence their approach to news coverage. Their instinct is to give the story, whatever the story may be, to the reporter, and to treat the photographer and his take as ancillary. It is rare that the photographer is thought of as a coequal newsgatherer, and rarer still that he is given the primary reporting responsibility.

This failure of confidence in the news photographer, this lack of vision where his thoroughly visual art is concerned, is an encumbrance that many American newspapers are saddled with—and they

DUANE BRALEY, MINNEAPOLIS STAR (THIRD PLACE, EDITORIAL ILLUSTRATION)

suffer for it, both graphically and editorially. As the hundreds of prize-winning photographs in this volume—augmented by thousands of near-winners, submitted to the Pictures of the Year competition by photojournalists from large and

small papers across the country—clearly suggest, the talent is there, in abundance. What is missing, too frequently, is the needed confidence, the breadth of vision. And, finally, an appreciation of the kind of editorial economy that a thousand-word picture affords.

Photography is potentially the most powerful—and generally the most underutilized—element in journalism. To appreciate the wisdom of the first observation—that photojournalism is compelling and persuasive—you need only think of any recent event in world history. Of the Spanish Civil War, for instance, or raising the flag at Iwo Jima, or John Fitzgerald Kennedy's funeral, or Kent State. What occurs to you, almost immediately, is that what you recollect is not written or spoken words—the lines, for example, from Senate Majority Leader Mike Mansfield's profoundly touching elegy-in-verse, delivered over

TOM HERDE, TRENTON TIMES (FIRST PLACE, EDITORIAL ILLUSTRATION)

ROB KINMONTH, (NEWPORT NEWS DAILY) PRESS-TIMES HERALD (SECOND PLACE, EDITORIAL ILLUSTRATION)

Kennedy's bier—but photographic images: the riderless horse with its back-turned stirrups; the hatless leaders of Western Europe walking solemnly behind the caisson. The emotions of a given moment, concentrated in images—photographic images.

To appreciate the wisdom of the second observation—that photojournalism is too often neglected—you need only study the pages of any American newspaper. What you discover, almost immediately, is that the more prestigious the paper, the less likely it is to give over precious editorial space to photographs, relying instead on first-class reporting from its correspondents to carry the full editorial load.

In this light it is especially noteworthy that a recent edition of the New York Times carried, in the space usually reserved for printed editorials, a large photograph of the fetid, flea-infested hold of a tramp

freighter, adrift somewhere in the South China Sea. The headline told us what we already suspected, namely that the hapless hordes crammed into the ship's hold were "boat people," refugees from the internecine strife in Cambodia and Vietnam—men, women and children who found life untenable at home and now find themselves unwelcome abroad. It was the photograph, however, and not the headline that told the true tale, more starkly and pitilessly than a printed editorial ever could. Here, before our own eyes, was the squalor, the degradation, and the sheer terror that even the best reporting from Southeast Asia had only been able to suggest, not convey. Here, without abstraction, without sentimentalizing, was actual human flotsam, adrift on a sea of indifference. And no such editorializing was needed to make the point. Just one picture.

The problem with a news pic-

ture—which is also its greatest virtue, of course—is that it gives you the event as it happened, innocent of editorializing. An editor can choose which picture he runs, naturally, and he can choose how he plays that picture. But he cannot choose what the picture says, nor can he alter its contents. In print, the plight of the "boat people" can be romanticized, sanitized, fictionalized, or politicized—and the value of photojournalism is that it strictly limits precisely this sort of specious editoralizing.

There is, however, a form of photojournalism—the editorial illustration—that does attempt to substantiate a specific point of view, that goes beyond the traditional task of photojournalism, which is simply to present what is, bereft of value judgments. Too often this brand of photojournalism is merely illustrative—reinforcing an editorial point that it could make, and possibly make better, on its own. But at its best, as in the examples seen here, editorial illustration can stand on its own as a photojournalistic device. Tom Herde's elegant photomontage (left) fuses the two durable symbols of Independence Day, Old Glory and the traditional Fourth of July picnic, into a single image that conveys warmth, wit, and humor with no sacrifice in patriotism. At top left Duane Braley offers an entire essay on the articulate body in two conjoined images. And in the arresting composition above, Rob Kinmonth makes a subtle but vital point about artistic collaboration in the performing arts with a directness and concision that the written word cannot match. Here is photojournalism that is not only powerful but well-employed.

THE EDITORS

7

FORM & TEXTURE

IN THEORY, photojournalists concern themselves with content, leaving studio photographers to deal with aesthetics. In practice, however, the two are all but indivisible: the best studio photographs raise questions that transcend their superficial glamor, and the best photojournalism is more than merely informative. Small wonder, then, that many of the best photographs submitted to the thirty-sixth annual Pictures of the Year competition should prove to be at once artfully composed and strikingly lit — attributes we traditionally associate with art photography, not photojournalism. Superior to most but typical of the best is *National Geographic* photographer Bill Weems's painterly portrait, opposite, of a pair of swans that he found floating on the still surface of the reflecting pool of the Lincoln Memorial in Washington, D.C. Here is an instance in which arresting image and dazzling color lend a certain highly refined, abstract elegance to what is only incidentally a record of two large water birds slowly bisecting the golden reflection of the national capital's famed obelisk, the Washington Monument.

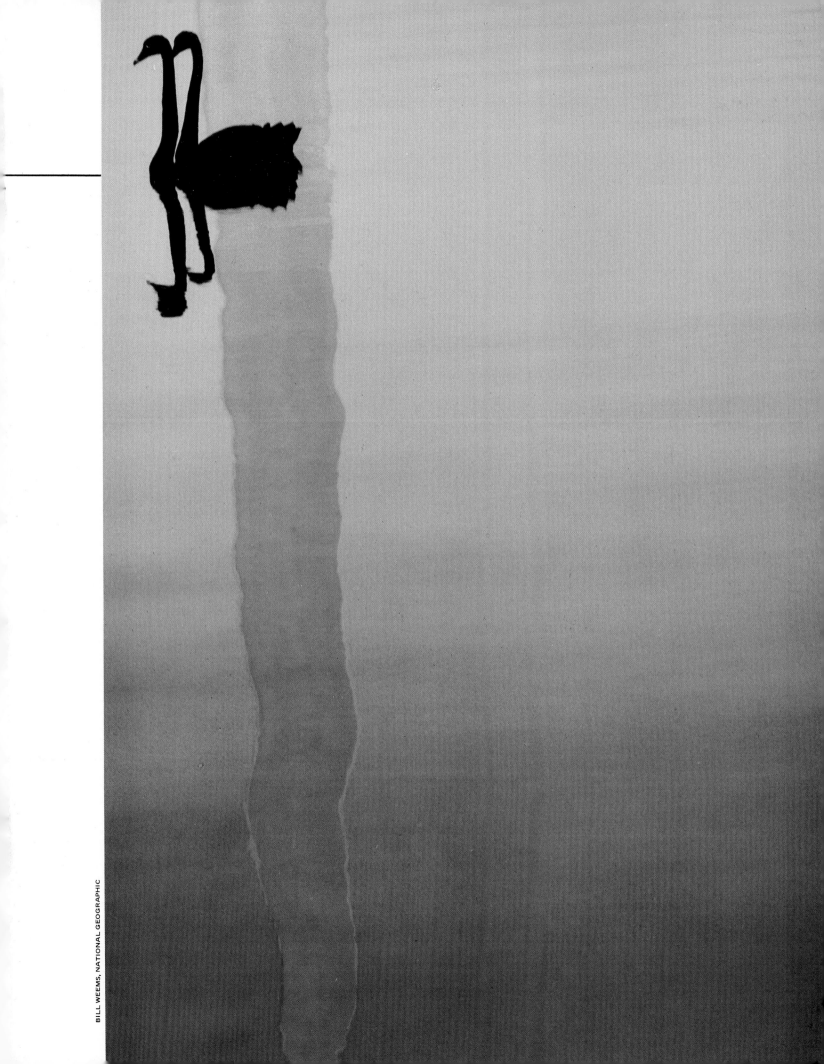

"I soared the sky on laughter-silvered wings...." The line is from a hymn familiar to Air Force pilots, but it might be every bit as logically invoked by this lone figure, piloting his hang-glider past a pastel sunset off the coast of Southern California. From this conspiracy of clouds and shoreline, photographer Barry Fitzsimmons has created a composition in soft colors and bold horizontals.

OVERLEAF: The scene is familiar, but the angle is not—and that transforms what might have been a rather ordinary shot of frame cottages lining a Massachusetts beach into a striking essay in light and shadow. We see the sea as the grey gulls do, and the angle turns the tide to tatting. And we see the houses as few owners do, with their architecture largely subordinated to their shadows.

BARRY FITZSIMMONS, SAN DIEGO UNION AND TRIBUNE

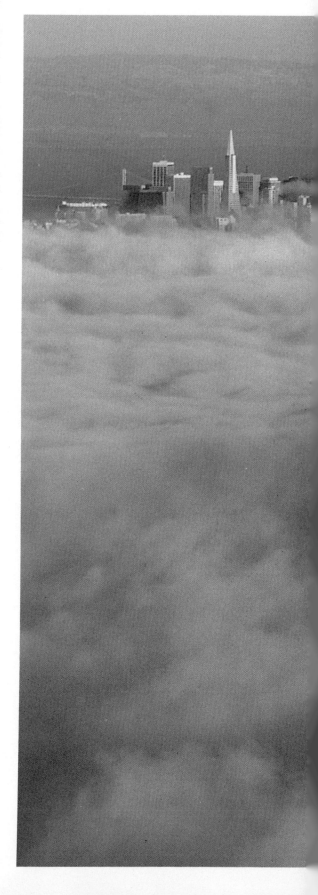

Magazine Photographer of the Year James A. Sugar recently settled in San Francisco, and his prize-winning portfolio is a valentine to his adopted city, which he clearly regards with the intense enthusiasm of a native. Seeing the Bay Area through unjaded eyes, he has given us a wholly fresh view of San Francisco's most-photographed monument, the Golden Gate Bridge, swaddled here in the bay's renowned fog. Above, the cormorants at nearby Point Lobos form a delicate tracery across the evening sky.

In discussing his film "2001, A Space Odyssey," director Stanley Kubrick once said that he had made the spaceship, rather than the men who inhabited it, the star of the movie because "technology is sexy." It is certainly true that pure technology has an elegance and appeal all its own, as these photographs indicate. Opposite: Light plays upon the sleek skin of a private plane as it hovers over a warp of landing lights. Below: Dirck Halstead's "jumbo jumble" of bottle noses, cargo doors and airline logos.

DIRCK HALSTEAD, TIME (FIRST PLACE, FEATURE PICTURE/MAG), ORIGINAL IN COLOR

17

Snow is nature's answer to high-contrast printing: it erases all topographical detail and throws nature into sharp relief. Like high-contrast printing, snow is extremely tricky to work with; it can undo the unwary photographer by flattening perspective and eliminating necessary detail. Two lensmen who have met this special challenge are Michael Coers, whose pale pastorale at left was taken the day after a record 14-inch snowfall in Goshen, Kentucky; and Dick Van Nostrand, whose overview below of a man with a snowblower shows him exhuming what looks for all the world like a plaster of Paris mock-up of an automobile.

DICK VAN NOSTRAND, THE BAY CITY (MICHIGAN) TIMES (SECOND PLACE, PICTORIAL)

MICHAEL COERS, COURIER-JOURNAL AND LOUISVILLE TIMES (HONORABLE MENTION, PICTORIAL)

DAVID HAUSAM, FREELANCE, UNIVERSITY OF MISSOURI

ABOVE: *The fairest measure of a photographer's "eye" is his ability to perceive beauty in the most mundane of objects—which is just what David Hausam reveals to us in this study of a tomato patch shrouded against the autumn's first frost. The elements could not be simpler—grass, tarp, stucco— but each is different in texture.*

RIGHT: Somehow, the quality of light that filters across these old, worn floorboards and pools beneath the simple, straightback chair is precisely what one would expect to encounter in the chancel of a country church—and Mark Sluder's view of a Pennsylvania church simultaneously confirms and exceeds our shared expectations.

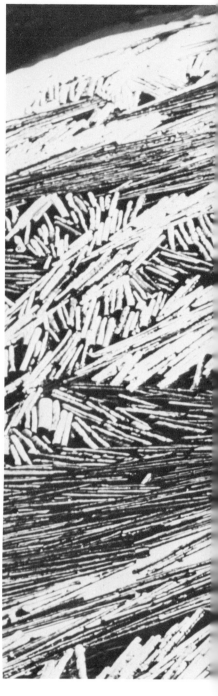

In the case of automobile tires it's not ashes to ashes but road-gripper to recap to reclaiming plant, where tired tires that have rolled their last are melted down, molded sound, and belted round—ready to hit the road again. While awaiting their moment of reincarnation, these road-slick radials and retired duo-plies have been stacked in interlaced tiers at a plant outside Dallas, Texas.

Chaos, under precisely the right circumstances, can assume a very special sort of order all its own—which is precisely what we find in David S. Boyer's prize-winning photograph above. The scene is a lumber company's holding pen, one filled to the rim with fresh-cut logs. The patterns here are random, but they are patterns nonetheless: a whirl, a sweep, two eddies—the shifting surface of a cellulose sea.

23

*Skiers call this method of ascent
(feet turned out, legs braced, and
elbows akimbo) the herringbone—
for the pattern it leaves behind
on the snow. In Erwin Gebhard's
photo, a hundred skiers ascending
a slope together form a larger,
more complicated pattern on the
snow—of skis, poles, articulated
limbs, and racing numerals.*

DAVID L. FINCH, DES MOINES REGISTER AND TRIBUNE

To suggest the faceless frenzy that is the start of any marathon race, photographer David L. Finch of the <u>Des Moines Register</u> chose a distant vantage, a long lens, and a slow shutter speed. The resultant picture appears to be undulating in sympathy with its straining subjects, who epitomize the familiar line "a sea of faces."

Look. Now, look again, for what you see and what you get are two rather different things in these two instances. A double-take is built into both these photographs, for both achieve a trompe l'oeil quality, albeit by very different means. John W. McDonough's print below, for instance, is not a worm's-eye view of the underside of a leaf. Rather, it's a condor's-eye view of a recently tilled farm, its furrows and roads reduced to delicate hatchwork. And as Richard Derk is quick to point out about the print opposite, he has not resorted to trick photography to produce the "inset." It was happenstance—and a missing pane of glass—that provided Derk with his remarkable two-in-one shot.

JOHN W. McDONOUGH, LOS ANGELES TIMES/SAN DIEGO (HONORABLE MENTION, PICTORIAL)

RICHARD DERK, CHICAGO DAILY NEWS (SECOND PLACE, NEWSPAPER PHOTOGRAPHER OF THE YEAR)

WORLD NEWS

ANDERSONVILLE, Dachau, Babi Yar, My Lai. To the list of obscure hamlets that have become synonymous with human suffering of the most brutal and senseless kind, we must now add Jonestown, Guyana. Little more than a jungle clearing and a clutch of tin-roofed sheds, Jonestown was a settlement without substance — until November 20, 1978, when the South American empire-in-exile of cult leader Jim Jones became the site of the largest mass suicide in history. The official tally was more than 900 dead — and tape-recorded evidence retrieved from the encampment suggested that not all the "suicides" were voluntary. One photographer, a veteran of the Vietnam and Indo-Pakistani wars and no stranger to carnage and catastrophe, confessed that Jonestown gave him the first nightmares of his career. Frank Johnston of the *Washington Post* was in the first group of photographers to reach the death site, and his prize-winning picture, opposite, of that grisly scene focuses on the fateful vat of cyanide-laced fruit punch and the empty syringes that became emblematic of the entire tragedy.

FRANK B. JOHNSTON, THE WASHINGTON POST (FIRST PLACE, NEWS PICTURE STORY)

Small children do not commit suicide—and hundreds of them died alongside the adults in Jamestown. The responsibility for their deaths—which must be regarded as murder—falls principally upon their distraught and misguided families, who forced the young to drink a deadly concoction of cyanide and fruit punch before imbibing the potion themselves. Jones's followers were, by and large, poor and ignorant—socially and emotionally disenfranchised people who were particularly receptive to his mesmerizing charlatanism and obedient to his warped will. Having very little to hold them back, they followed Jones to Guyana when he fled there from San Francisco. And having even less to hold on to in South America, they followed his increasingly unbalanced orders there—even unto death.

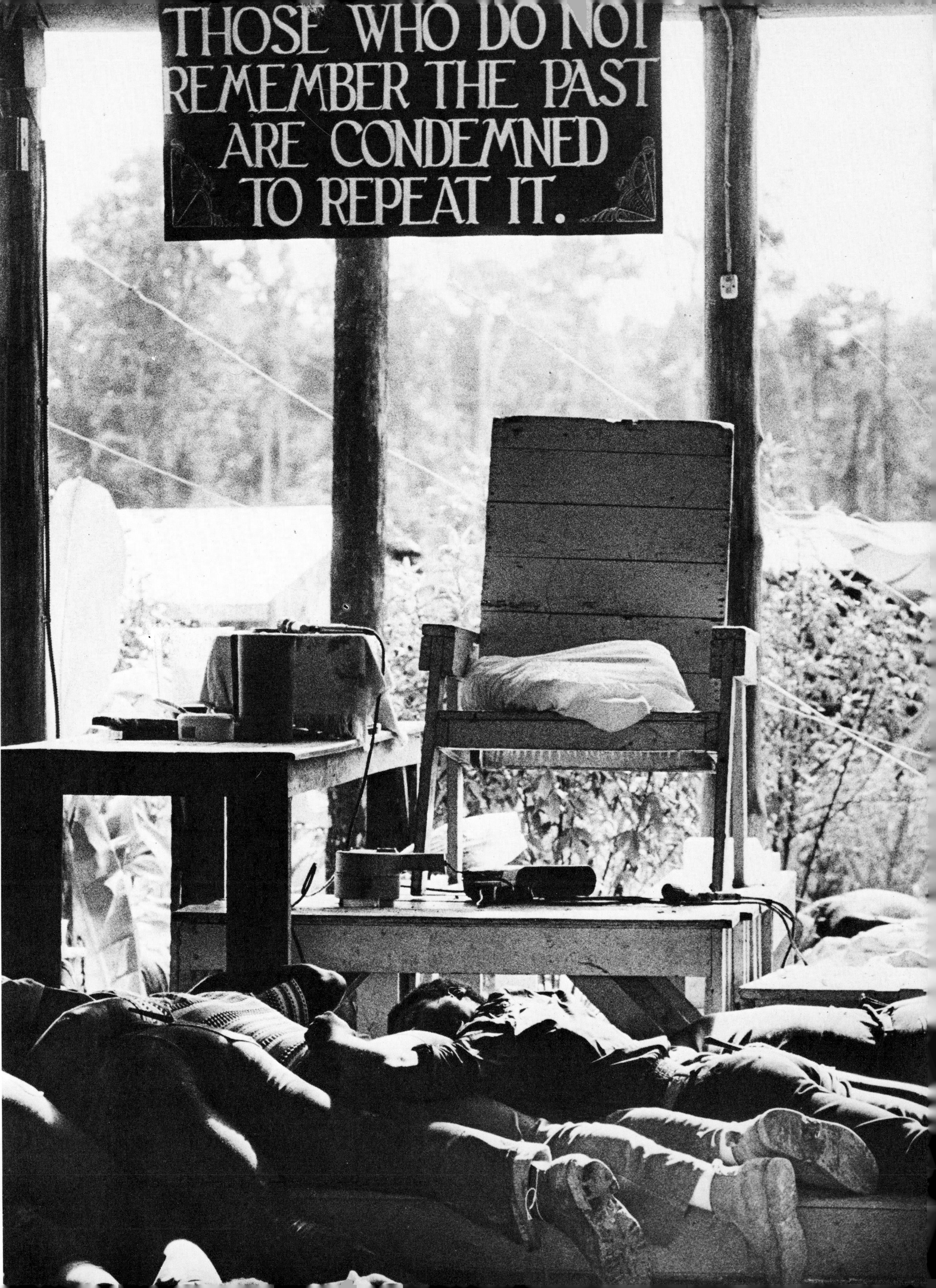
THOSE WHO DO NOT
REMEMBER THE PAST
ARE CONDEMNED
TO REPEAT IT.

FRANK B. JOHNSTON, THE WASHINGTON POST

The special irony of the motto posted above Jones's makeshift throne (left) is that George Santayana's sage advice should have been in plain sight—and so plainly ignored. Bizarre quasi-religious sects are not new to history, after all, nor are megalomaniacal, self-appointed saviors. Even death cults and mass suicide have historical precedent. But the hapless residents of Jonestown did not remember the lessons of history—if indeed they had ever learned them—and so they were condemned to repeat the past. And because the victims of Jones's burgeoning paranoia were American citizens, it fell to the U.S. Army to retrieve their bloated corpses, pack them in aluminum caskets (right), and return them to the States for burial.

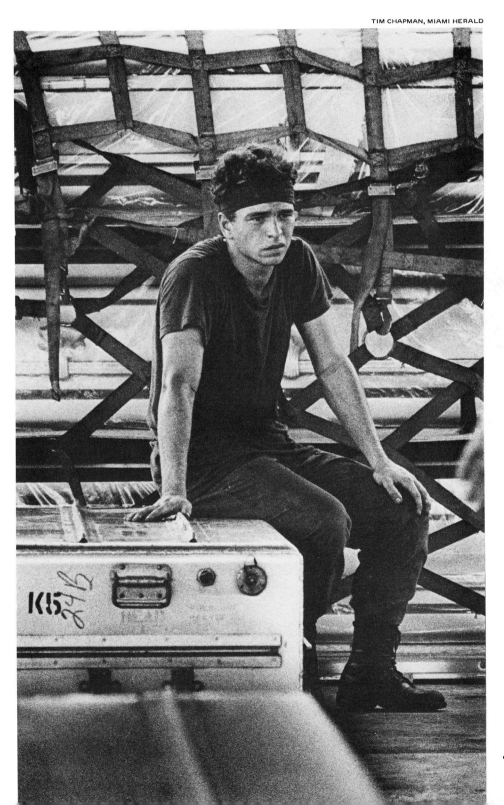

The long shadow that fell across Italian politics in 1978 was red, not black—cast by the so-called Red Brigade, a terrorist group that gave the language a new verb, "knee-capping," to identify those attacks intended only to maim, not to kill. A sterner fate awaited the Red Brigade's most prominent victim, ex-premier Aldo Moro, whose life was a pawn brokered by the terrorists in a game of political cat-and-mouse that lasted for weeks—and ended, above, on a busy public thoroughfare in downtown Rome on May 9.

Dissent of a far more civilized sort marked Canadian politics in 1978, as citizens found themselves confronting the most serious threat to national unity in the country's history. Champions of French-Canadian separatism argued for the establishment of a secessionist state of Quebec, thus putting Prime Minister Pierre Elliot Trudeau (above, addressing a gathering in his home riding of Montreal) in the uncomfortable—and ultimately untenable—position of defending his homeland against his heritage.

LEFT: *The political action that created a homeland for the Jews after World War II inevitably displaced other peoples, first among them Palestinians, who have called the land that is modern Israel their home for as long as the Biblical tribes of Israel have. Excluded from the Camp David summit meeting, which was certain to affect their future, Palestinians took to the streets in protest.*

BELOW: *Nicaraguan President Anastasio Somoza Debayle was the United States' oldest friend in Latin America and a longtime recipient of American largesse. And so it followed that, when less friendly Nicaraguans rose in open rebellion against the Somoza dictatorship, he should use U.S.-trained men to quell the rising. It proved possible to clap the lid on, but not to keep the pot from eventually boiling over.*

JOE ELBERT, MIAMI HERALD

In the end, only the longer prespective of history will be able to reveal which upheaval proved the greater for Iran in 1978—the earthquake that claimed 16,000 lives in the small eastern community of Tabas (above) or the religious revolution (right) that toppled the autocratic shah in Teheran.

If President Jimmy Carter's face seems suffused with pride and joy, those feelings are not misplaced, for thanks in large measure to his efforts, two historical enemies— Egyptian President Anwar Sadat (back to camera) and Israeli Prime Minister Menachem Begin—have signed a brace of agreements that represent a major step toward ending the Middle East conflict.

NATIONAL NEWS

IN ONE SENSE the flag-draped figure opposite is a cultural hold-over from the sixties, for Richard Derk found him swaddled in Old Glory at a Yippie reunion in Chicago. But in another sense he is a symbol of the times, for dissent and confrontation are still very much a part of American life. So much so, in fact, that the editors have chosen to devote the first half of this section to a photographic review of the causes and crusades that made news last year — from women's rights, gay rights, and First Amendment rights to protests against nuclear proliferation and court-mandated busing to achieve school desegregation. The list is as diverse as it is long, and it includes such strange bedfellows as the Native American — whose cause has widespread public support — and the American Nazi Party — whose very existence is anathema to many. National News also includes contributions from John McDonough, who spotlights the plight of the illegal alien (pages 60-61), and J.G. Domke, who records the final, tragic clash between members of the Philadelphia commune MOVE and local police (pages 56-59).

44

Having honed her rhetorical skills on a campaign biography of Barry Goldwater that could still serve, some fifteen years later, as a casebook for students of the sly innuendo and the slippery syllogism, Phyllis Schlafly (left) has turned her formidable forensic force on the Equal Rights Amendment— which, she warns listeners, could lead to universal conscription (which Israel has) and to alimony payments to divorced husbands (which one New York woman is already paying). The merit of such arguments aside, these considerations are ancillary to the true purpose of the E.R.A., which is intended to protect the rights of women in the job market—a group that includes nearly half of all American wives. Below, the hard-working wives of three Presidents—Lady Bird Johnson, Rosalynn Carter, and Betty Ford—join one of the nation's leading spokespersons for women's rights, Bella Abzug, at the First National Women's Conference in Houston, Texas. As part of the opening ceremony, the trio of First Ladies lofts a torch that has been carried by more than 2,000 runners from Seneca Falls, New York, site of the Women's Rights Convention of 1848.

DIANA MARA HENRY, FREELANCE

JAMES L. BATES, (ABERDEEN, WASHINGTON) DAILY WORLD

For protest to become policy, it must first engage the public's sympathy—which is precisely what happened to the No Nukes movement when it acquired its first martyr in Karen Silkwood. Silkwood died under mysterious circumstances en route to a rendezvous with a <u>New York Times</u> reporter—to whom she allegedly intended to deliver evidence of radiation hazards at a plant run by her employer, Kerr-McGee. Soon the opponents of nuclear proliferation were marching into battle under her banner (left). Then came Three Mile Island (and its uncanny cinematic precursor, "The China Syndrome")...and suddenly millions of Americans who had never heard of Karen Silkwood got her message. The anti-nuclear protests grew in number and impact, and what had once been erroneously described as a "refuge for old antiwar radicals" like the white-thatched man at right, jailed for joining an anti-nuke sit-in, became a protest movement of international scope—and one with widespread public sympathy.

Last year students at Kent State rallied to protest the construction of a gymnasium on the site where four of their

predecessors were slain by National Guardsmen in 1970. This time authorities responded with tear gas, not bullets.

If there is any right that we regard as inalienable, it is the right to speak our minds, when and where we please. The Founding Fathers put free speech first on the Bill of Rights, and the courts have been ardent in their defense of so-called First Amendment rights ever since. Occasionally, however, the rights of one citizen collide head on with those of another. Such a collision occurred last year when *New* *York* *Times* reporter Myron Farber's right to protect his news sources ran headlong into Dr. Mario Jascalevich's right to a fair trial. Farber (left) spent forty days in jail, and the notorious "Dr. X" went free. In the case of the chairperson of the President's Advisory Committee on Women, the conflict was between Bella Abzug's right to have her say and President Carter's right to take umbrage. She did; he did; and she lost her post.

ROBERT A. NANDELL, DES MOINES REGISTER

Voltaire's oft-repeated line, "I disapprove of what you say, but I will defend to the death your right to say it," expresses the very essence of the American Ideal. In theory, all liberty-loving citizens concur with Voltaire; freedom of speech is a sacred Constitutional guarantee, after all. In practice, however, we sometimes find ourselves hard-pressed to stand with Voltaire—especially when we disapprove completely of what is being said. This ethical dilemma is one that millions of Americans had to confront last summer when the American Nazi Party announced its intention to march through the streets of Skokie, Illinois, a community with a substantial population of Nazi concentration camp survivors. With so many deaths to their credit, the Nazis found few latter-day Voltaires willing to defend to the death their right to march. Party leader Frank Collin, posed formally above with a 13-year-old member of the Nazi Youth Front, was permitted to stage a small, court-mandated rally (right), but not in Skokie.

The Bible is the work of many hands, and consequently it is possible to find a passage in it somewhere that will support any point of view. The disturbing thing about Bible-thumping bigots is not their zeal—which, if it were directed elsewhere, might be regarded as righteousness— but their zealous determination to impose their interpretation of the Scriptures on a nation founded by men fleeing religious intolerance of precisely that sort. It is civil law, not the Book of Leviticus, that governs relations between consenting adults in this country—but try telling that to Anita Bryant.

WILLIAM STEINMETZ, THE PHILADELPHIA INQUIRER

NORMAN Y. LONO, PHILADELPHIA DAILY NEWS (THIRD PLACE, NEWS PICTURE STORY)

J.G. DOMKE, THE PHILADELPHIA INQUIRER

From the beginning it was a muddled situation. A group of dissident blacks had set up what they described as a back-to-nature commune—known by the acronym MOVE—in an abandoned Philadelphia tenement. Police sought to evict them, but to no avail, and in the ensuing weeks of jurisdictional stalemate the commune found itself virtually cut off from the outside world. Negotiations with Delbert Africa,

self-styled leader of MOVE, came to a bitter conclusion on a dog day in August—in an exchange of gunfire that left one officer dead and several others wounded. Under threat of renewed attack, the commune capitulated and women and children emerged (left). They were followed by Africa himself, who encountered the full fury of a police force that was already notorious for its brutality (below, left to right).

OVERLEAF: Except for the bricks and the bluejeans, the scene could easily be Equatorial Africa, so convincingly does this picture capture the vaguely articulated "back-to-nature" aspect of the MOVE commune. The elaborately plaited hair and clinging babes seem to belong to another century and another continent. But the pavement is a street in Philadelphia, torn up by the pressure of fire hoses.

J.G. DOMKE, THE PHILADELPHIA INQUIRER

NORMAN Y. LONO, PHILADELPHIA DAILY NEWS (THIRD PLACE, NEWS PICTURE STORY)

NORMAN Y. LONO, PHILADELPHIA DAILY NEWS (THIRD PLACE, NEWS PICTURE STORY)

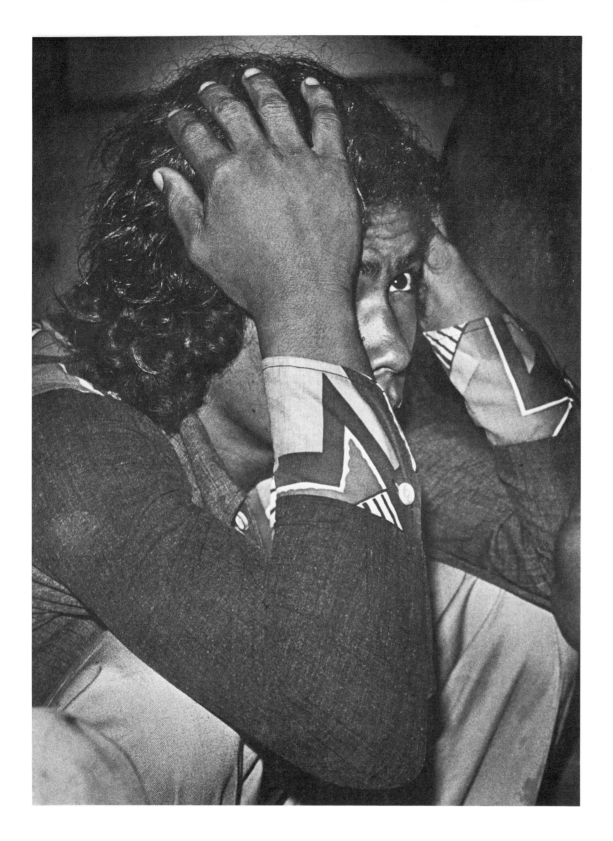

"Welcome, welcome, emigrante," goes the opening line of one of Buffy Sainte-Marie's loveliest folk songs—and although the sentiment is admirable the words are often false, at least when spoken by Tio Sam, as many Mexicans choose to identify their "uncle" to the north. Laborers looking for better wages and a better life have crossed the border in untold numbers in the past decade, and millions of illegal aliens now dwell north of the border, up California way. Those who make the trip without being apprehended—and hundreds do every week—are absorbed by the barrio of East Los Angeles and exploited in the fields of the valleys beyond. For those who fail to slip by the Border Patrol, there is arrest (above) and forced return to Mexico (right)... to wait for another, less carefully watched freight train bound for the north.

A feature of American politics in the past decade has been the emergence of the special interest group as a potent force in the shaping of governmental policy. The will of the majority, it often seems, is being replaced by the willfulness of certain small, vocal, and well-organized minorities. Politicians are rightly wary of such groups, which can turn out hundreds of protestors or thousands of voters, as the occasion demands. Take a conciliatory stand on abortion—and suffer the fate of the Senator from Iowa. Or investigate the Moonies—and go the way of the Representative from neighboring Minnesota. In recent years the smallest and least vocal segments of society have taken their cue from the more strident, and the result is anti-busing marches led by working-class mothers (left) and demonstrations for Indian rights held within hailing distance of the White House itself.

San Franciscans have long prided themselves on living in the "city that knows how"—a motto that has always had purely positive connotations. At least until last November, when the city was obliged to learn how to mourn— for a progressive mayor and an openly homosexual city supervisor, assassinated by a former colleague whom they had opposed in his efforts to reclaim a council seat he had recently resigned. Their names, respectively, were Moscone, Milk and White. The city wept for the first two, and eventually tried the third for murder. The verdict was manslaughter, the sentence negligible, and the reaction predictable: again the city wept, and this time it raged as well.

During his long career in the
Senate, Hubert H. Humphrey
was known as a scrapper, and he
fought his last battle—against
invasive bladder cancer—with
characteristic tenacity. He lost that
battle, but over the years he had
won many others in the Congress,
and so, in death, he assumed
a prominent place in a very special
pantheon of American heroes—
those who shaped the course of
national history as fully as any
President, but without ever wearing
the mantle. To mark the Happy
Warrior's passing, those who had
worn the mantle—or hoped to
wear it—turned out for a memorial
service in the nation's capital.
Mourners included, from left to
right: former President Richard M.
Nixon, making a rare public
appearance; erstwhile First Lady
Betty Ford and her husband
Gerald; ex-Veep Nelson
Rockefeller, standing directly
behind Rosalynn and Jimmy
Carter; Humphrey's widow, Muriel;
the Mondales and the Kissingers;
and Lady Bird Johnson.

KENT KOBERSTEEN, MINNEAPOLIS TRIBUNE (HONORABLE MENTION, GENERAL NEWS)

BRYAN K. GRIGSBY, GAINESVILLE SUN (SECOND PLACE, GENERAL NEWS)

As convicted murderer Bennie Demps heard the judge pronounce him guilty of yet another murder—this one of a fellow inmate at the Rayford State Prison in Florida—Demps turned to his lawyer and grinned, his smirk a sharp counterpoint to the grim group of guards and legal counsels who witnessed the sentencing. Standing next to the judge, photographer Bryan Grigsby recorded this scene during the state of Florida's highly controversial "camera in the courtroom" experiment.

The night they raided the worst little whorehouse in Long Beach, Leo Hetzel tagged along. What the police found—and Hetzel photographed—was a belligerent owner; two dozen sheepish patrons, most of them illegal aliens; and two overworked prostitutes, both from Honduras and neither in possession of immigration papers. As the police burst in the front door, the owner ducked out the back and a chase ensued. The busted proprietor wound up with a cut on his nose (above).

RICHARD DERK, CHICAGO SUN-TIMES

CHRISTOPHER G. JOHNS, TOPEKA CAPITAL-JOURNAL (NEWSPAPER PHOTOGRAPHER OF THE YEAR)

When the Chicago police arrived to evict the couple at left from their South Side residence, the harassed pair threatened to shoot—and not just the men in blue but, for good measure, their own children as well. After an hour of fruitless negotiation the police decided that prudence was the better part of valor and withdrew, promising to come back when tempers had cooled.

Inevitably, some of the men who carry sidearms in the course of their work die by them, a fact their wives recognize without ever really reconciling themselves to it. When a Kansas state trooper named O'Brien was killed in the line of duty, his young wife was stoic—until she encountered one of her murdered husband's colleagues (above), and her reserve gave way to grief.

ALL: MIMI FULLER, CINCINNATI POST (SECOND PLACE, NEWS PICTURE STORY)

It was one of those perfect spring days—a clear blue sky and a warm sun shining with the promise of coming summer. But darkness seemed to descend over bucolic Washington Park when Cincinnati photographer Mimi Fuller came upon a nine-year-old boy beating a fifty-three-year-old wino as he slept on the grass (far left, above). While Patrolman Richard Gross collared the boy (near left) and locked him up in the cage-like confines of his patrol car (far left, below), the victim, Jack Young, was taken to the hospital suffering from facial injuries. Although he initially denied any wrongdoing, the frightened youth broke down and began to weep copiously (above) after he was charged with assault. Incidentally, photographer Fuller went to victim Young's aid immediately after the first picture in this sequence was made.

Depending on how you looked at it, the Mirage Tavern (below) was either an inspired piece of investigative journalism...or the journalistic equivalent of police entrapment. The bar, you see, was owned and operated by the <u>Chicago Sun-Times</u> for the express purpose of exposing rampant graft among city building inspectors. There were plumbing and wiring violations aplenty at the Mirage (near right and far right, above), and Chicago inspectors had no trouble finding them.

But then, instead of shutting down the egregiously ill-managed establishment, they merely opened their pockets (far right, below) and closed their eyes. The ethics of the paper's approach to newsgathering disturbed a number of journalists, among them members of the Pulitzer Committee, which denied the <u>Sun-Times</u> a prize many felt it had earned. But there was no question that the newspaper's daring enterprise served the citizens of the Windy City well indeed.

ALL: JIM FROST, CHICAGO SUN-TIMES

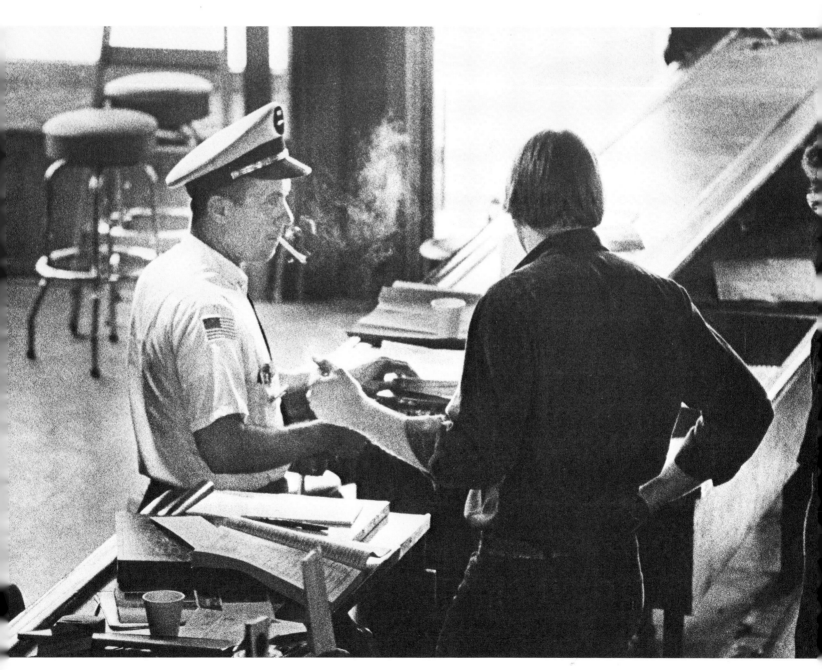

It was, in a very real sense, a year
of both triumph and tragedy
for the aviation industry. The
tragedy was due to human error:
PSA Flight 182, in-bound
to San Diego's municipal
airport with 135 on board,
collided with a small private
aircraft and burst into flames.
"We're going down," was
the terse message from pilot
to control tower—and Hans
Wendt froze the final, stricken
descent on film (left). The
triumph was due to human
ingenuity: 50,000 employees
of 5,000 aerospace companies
worked for five years to produce
the space shuttle, the ungainly
but eminently practical craft
seen, at lower right, riding
piggyback on a larger 747. Once
launched, the shuttle is capable of
suborbital flight, space flight,
and—most importantly—return
flight. Unlike ill-fated Skylab,
the shuttle can reenter the
earth's atmosphere and glide to
a safe landing on an airstrip
designed especially for it.

Nearly five years ago, Robert Fox climbed a catwalk to rescue three fellow-workers who had been overcome by hydrogen sulphide gas at the Mobil Oil refinery in Joliet, Illinois. Two of the three workers recovered, but Fox, for his pains, became a vegetable, victim of the deadly gas which, if inhaled, goes through the lungs into the bloodstream, paralyzing the nerve centers of the brain. "Sometimes I have a glimmer of hope he will come out of it," says wife Donna (right), "but it's a fantasy, I guess."

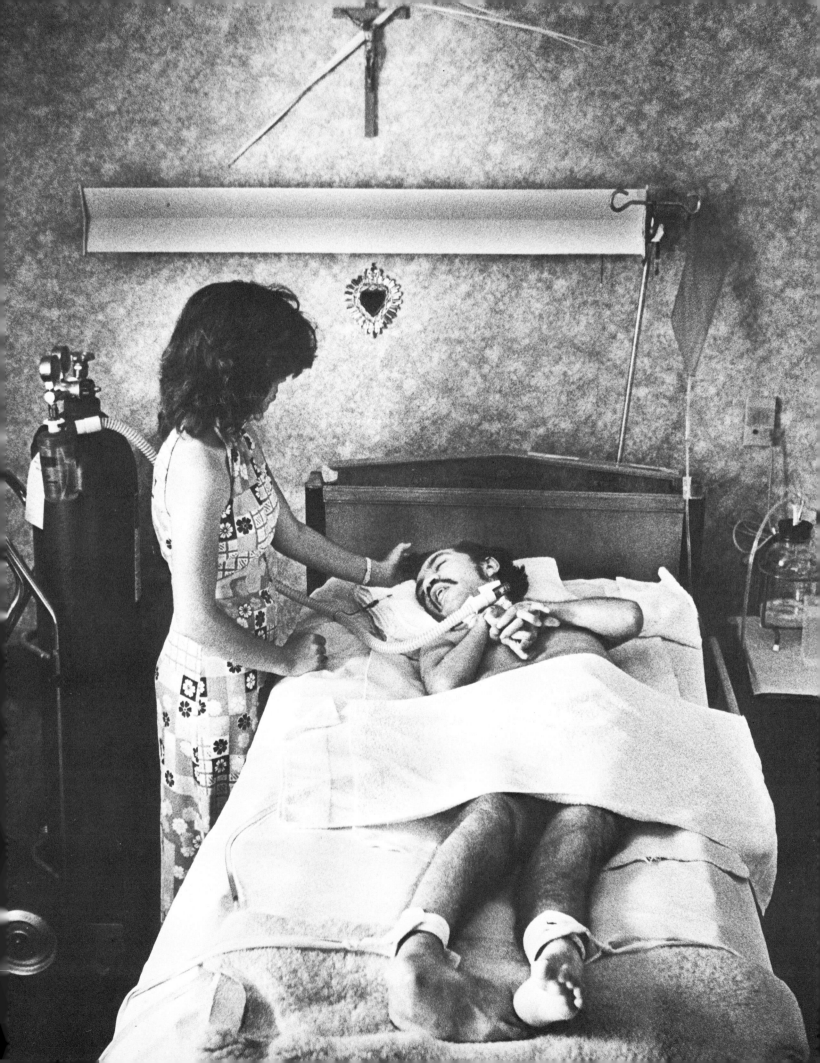

"It was a cursed snowfall that gave central Missouri its whitest Easter since 1920," says David Walters of the natural disaster he photographed in and around Cedar City last spring. Cursed because the snow soon melted—and threatened to inundate the farms of men like Bill Ansel (near right). "Sandbagging crews worked through the night to contain overflowing creeks and tributaries," Walters reports. They then turned their attention to the levee that was Cedar City's only flood protection. Before the waters crested, much of the flat, fertile farmland around the city was under water.

ALL: DAVID WALTERS, MIAMI HERALD

OVERLEAF: Fifteen-year-old Allen Pinet was one of the volunteers who worked around the clock to turn back the flood tide that threatened the farming community of Cedar City, Missouri. The waters rose steadily for a week, but thanks to the efforts of Pinet and others, the sandbag dikes did too. And when the waters finally fell and Allen could at last relax, the damage done proved to be slight.

Given a scant thirty minutes' notice of his assignment—just time enough to round up his cameras and several rolls of film—Cramer Gallimore joined the Army rescue teams being airlifted into the beleaguered city of Boston in the wake of one of the most disastrous blizzards in its history. Gallimore's take included the view at left of a buried parking lot at Civil Defense headquarters in suburban Framingham, bathed in an eerie glow, and the half-submerged caravan of cars at right.

BILL TYNAN, SYRACUSE NEWSPAPERS

The driving snowstorm that led to this fiery crash on a slick stretch of Syracuse, New York freeway also transformed the scene into an ersatz Jackson Pollock canvas, with gigantic snowflakes partially obscuring the crumpled, flame-engulfed wreck in the foreground and the well-bundled spectators and their temporarily abandoned cars, visible in the background.

And always there are fires—a staple of photojournalism and a fact of life for as long as men have erected shelters over their heads. The shelter, in the case below, is a mobile home, gutted by a blaze that charred the interior and blistered the exterior. At right, a Miami fireman picks his way through the ruins of a suburban home, his path illumined by light spilling through blackened roofbeams.

JOHN H. WHITE, CHICAGO SUN-TIMES (HONORABLE MENTION, NEWS PICTURE STORY)

Fire may well be the single worst enemy of the urban poor, for it preys upon their neighborhoods with terrible regularity and awesome effect. (New York's South Bronx, for example, has been more thoroughly devastated by arson than Dresden was by concerted Allied firebombing in World War II.) Sometimes the cause is arson; sometimes, mere carelessness—but always the effect is the same: the ill-housed are left homeless, and those with few possessions find themselves with fewer still. Often this loss is not measured in property alone, for tenement conflagrations also claim lives— too often small lives.

In an attempt to salvage what
remains of the King David
Baptist Church, located
on Chicago's South Side,
fire fighters train gushing
arcs of water on its smoking
belfry and ruined nave. Some
135 firemen and more than
40 pieces of equipment
responded to the alarm one
Sunday morning in April
of last year. By the time they
arrived, flickering flames lit
the dawn sky; and before
those flames could be brought
under control, much of the
church had been reduced to
blackened timbers and ash.

No, fella, it's not sunstroke: the Marines <u>have</u> landed. Their presence doesn't seem to faze this sunbather, however—and no wonder. He's an underwater demolitions expert who helped plan this landing exercise.

ROBERT LACHMAN, LOS ANGELES TIMES (SECOND PLACE, FEATURE PICTURE)

PEOPLE

THE FIRST SUBJECT of photography is people. Portrait and Personality is odds-on the largest category in each POY competition, and the entries tend to be of the highest quality — which makes the task of winnowing winners from the work submitted an especially arduous one for the contest's panel of judges. What remains is a truly distinguished group of portraits. It includes a host of famous faces (among them that of actor-environmentalist Robert Redford, immediately recognizable despite his stubble, on page 99) and a smaller number of infamous ones (such as Nixon Resurrectus, page 106, or porcine, glowering Bert Lance, page 110). But the bulk of the portraits — and the best of them — are of ordinary men and women, who can communicate far more directly with us because we bring no particular preconceptions or prejudices to our examination of their features. An exquisite example of this latter group is veteran AP photographer Eddie Adams's study, opposite, in shades of sepia, of a low-caste Untouchable whom Adams encountered at an open-air bazaar in the Indian city of Bihar.

JONATHAN BLAIR, NATIONAL GEOGRAPHIC (HONORABLE MENTION, PORTRAIT/MAG)

A former rodeo cowboy, A.C. Ekker (left) now operates an outfitting service called Outlaw Trails, which guides parties through an area that once was home to the most notorious desperadoes of the Wild West. Their number included the Red Sash Gang, Jesse and Frank James, Big Nose George Parrott, the famed Butch Cassidy, and his partner, the Sundance Kid, a wily rogue who was transformed into a romantic legend by actor Robert Redford (below). Redford, who makes his home in the Utah mountains, recently retraced a 600-mile stretch of the Outlaw Trail, which once ran all the way from northern Montana to the Mexican border. Along the way he dropped rein at such legendary hangouts as Hole-in-the-Wall, a one-time refuge for killers and thieves, and shot the breeze—but only the breeze—with codgers who still remember the territory as it was in the bad old days.

JONATHAN BLAIR, NATIONAL GEOGRAPHIC (HONORABLE MENTION, FEATURE PICTURE STORY/MAG)

SISSE BRIMBERG, NATIONAL GEOGRAPHIC (FIRST PLACE, FEATURE PICTURE STORY/MAG)

Toiling in the fields is minimal hardship for the Canadian farm boy at left. In stature he's knee-high to a grasshopper, but the satisfaction of working the fields during the harvest season gives him a giant-sized glow. With his raggedy straw hat and insouciant grin, he has the look of a supremely contented latter-day Johnny Appleseed.

Autumn finds the young apple-picker above toiling ten-hour days alongside his parents and his four brothers and sisters in Washington State's Yakima Valley. Although many migrants are illegal aliens—an estimated 11,000 of whom help harvest each season's crop—growers insist that "the valley wouldn't get picked without them."

Slumped on a stool in his renowned Long Island studio— a great, open, airy space that the visitor feels is constantly filled with sunlight and sea breezes— painter Willem de Kooning spends hours on end contemplating his current work, usually perched atop old paint cans. At 74, this foremost figure in the Abstract Expressionist movement is still evolving; his latest canvases burst with color and vitality, revealing afresh the sensuous side of the painter's nature.

With the dramatic debut of the East Building of the National Gallery of Art in Washington, D.C., architect I.M. Pei (right) added the center gem to the diadem of public buildings he has designed over the last two decades. Pei claims that his triangular triumph, nearly a decade in the works, was "the most difficult piece of land I've ever worked with." The architect's solution: interlocking trapezoids of space and light, perfectly fitted to the structure's wedge-shaped plot.

102

Making his first public appearance since his resignation, deposed President Nixon was moved to give this fervent salute during the playing of the National Anthem and pledge to the flag. The place was the tiny Kentucky town of Hayden, where townspeople turned out in droves to have a look at the former Chief Executive.

RIGHT: Philadelphia mayor Frank L. Rizzo was defending the police department against charges of brutality when Norman Lono caught this scowl of disgust. "He always grimaces," says Lono, who covered the Mayor for over two years and was a frequent witness to Rizzo's stormy bouts with the press.

R. NORMAN MATHENY, THE CHRISTIAN SCIENCE MONITOR

For David Warren, the chance to take Senator Edward Kennedy's picture was a singular thrill. "It's the first—and only—time I've photographed him," observes Warren, who caught Kennedy making a campaign speech for former basketball star and Senate hopeful Bill Bradley. (Bradley won.) On assignment last summer, Arthur Grace caught New York Senator Daniel Patrick Moynihan (near left) in an uncharacteristically stationary pose. "He's not someone who will sit and pose," claims Grace. "You've got to be quick. There's a problem simply keeping up with the man." Keeping up with President Carter was Norman Matheny's assignment. The photo above may look like a studied portrait, but it was taken during a welcoming ceremony on the South Lawn of the White House for Rumanian president Nicolae Ceausescu last April. "Some photographers try to get the President with his face contorted in some strange way," comments Matheny, "but I get a kick out of showing the man as he might actually want himself to be seen."

FORCE

The indomitable Miz Lillian (above) was listening to—what else?—a politician's speech during a picnic in New Haven when Ken Randolph snapped her weathered face. After the picnic, the President's mother departed for—natch—another political event. Another dedicated Carter campaigner, Rosalynn, was caught off guard (right) during a grueling tour through Cook County, Illinois, on behalf of Senate hopeful Alex Smith. Comments photographer Richard Derk, "I wanted to show the First Lady as a tired human being, regardless of who she is. Photographers always like to go for those universal emotions."

RICHARD DERK, CHICAGO SUN-TIMES

GARY E. FONG, SAN FRANCISCO CHRONICLE (HONORABLE MENTION, PORTRAIT)

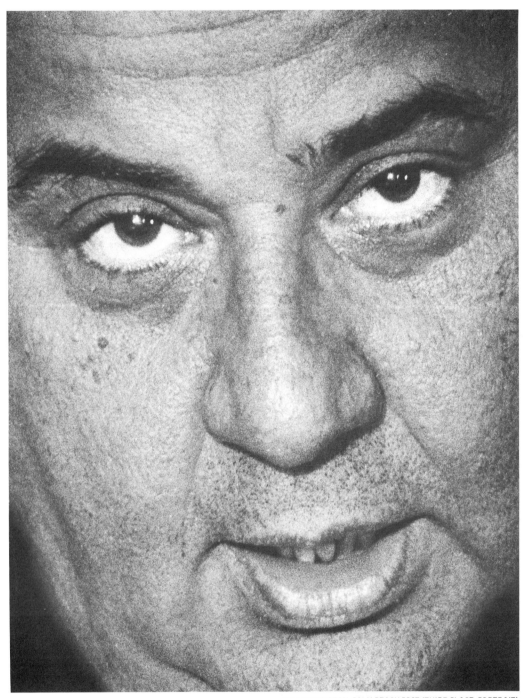

PAT PARTINGTON, PALM BEACH POST (THIRD PLACE, PORTRAIT)

Most people accept taxes with once-a-year whimpers, but for California tax fighter Howard Jarvis, they're something to scream about. The feisty reformer, who is the co-author of his state's controversial Proposition 13, was caught in a moment of fury (left) at a debate held in San Mateo County. The world of finance is also of prime concern to Bert Lance (right) these days. The guest speaker at a businessmen's lunch in Palm Beach, Florida, Lance felt obliged to open his remarks with a joke—which no one found funny. He glanced down at his notes, and "when he raised his head, I nailed him," relates Pat Partington. "I don't remember what the joke was—but it wasn't funny."

At 84, Alberta Hunter has made a comeback. The jazz and blues singer belts out ballads and blues twice nightly, six times a week, at a Greenwich Village club called The Cookery. The one-time toast of cafes from Chicago to Cairo was rediscovered at a party given by famed cafe singer Bobby Short for another legend, Mabel Mercer. Says Hunter of her comeback: "When I got down here, I had no idea what was going to come out of my mouth. I hadn't sung one note in twenty years."

When Rev. Ralph Abernathy came to St. Petersburg, Florida, in 1968, he vowed, "We're gonna stay here until the walls crack, segregation crumbles, and the garbage men get their jobs back." A decade later, some walls have tumbled and the garbage men have got their jobs back—but there's still a long way to go, the black leader claims. Abernathy offered this assessment at a recent press conference, and Steve Dozier was there to record the event.

These days, a celebrity without
a cause célèbre is like a rally
without Jane Fonda—and Yul
Brynner is no exception. In
reel and stage life, his most
famous role has been that of
the mercurial and dynamic King
of Siam; offstage, Mr. Brynner's
Romany blood has led him to
champion the cause of the world's
10 million gypsies. Brynner
was caught in this exuberant
pose by Suzanne Vlamis. "He
was very warm and intelligent,"
says Vlamis, "and his smile
was devastating."

Cat-lady Eartha Kitt has been called a lot of things, but shy has never been one of them. While having her photo snapped in a Broadway dressing room before going onstage in "Timbuktu!" the volatile Ms. Kitt played with her two dogs, sang, and contorted herself into yoga positions. "Maybe she was trying to psych herself up," suggests photographer Karen Wiles, who says of the formidable entertainer: "She comes across as intimidating, but she really isn't. There's just something about her." Indeed.

DERIS A. JEANNETTE, LOS ANGELES TIMES

Two legendary stars—one shining
as brightly as ever, the other one
fading fast. Few public figures
have had their physical decline
recorded in as graphic detail
as did the late John Wayne. Here,
he waves to fans from the backyard of his Newport Beach
home after returning from one
of his bouts of open-heart
surgery. While most of the press
were stationed on boats in the
harbor, Deris Jeannette was
able to get this exclusive. Her
approach? "I talked my way
through his house and into the
backyard." Adulation was also the
theme of the hour as 3,000 fans
paid homage to Bette Davis at
the Terrace Theater in Long Beach
during a retrospective of her
films last spring. Dressed in a
lavender gown, the 70-year-old
Ms. Davis strode onstage to answer
questions from the sold-out
audience. Although some film
buffs came to view clips from
Ms. Davis's 47-year career,
which began with "Cabin in the
Sky" in 1931, most came to
see and hear the legend in action.
With wit that has not been
dulled by years, the two-time
Oscar winner parried questions
with enviable ease.

The occasion was Zubin Mehta's farewell performance as conductor of the Los Angeles Philharmonic. "It was a very emotional evening," relates photographer Tony Barnard. But the flamboyant conductor—who recently left the wilds of the West for the top job at the New York Philharmonic—has not entirely forsaken West for East: he's returned to Los Angeles several times since his departure to serve as guest conductor. "This was his last official performance," stresses Barnard, "and because of that, it was reviewed with more interest." East or West, these photographs declare, Mehta's magnetism shines.

TONY BARNARD, LOS ANGELES TIMES

When the Rolling Stones came to Cleveland last summer, some 80,000 dauntless fans turned out in spite of the rain. Stones star Mick Jagger whipped off his shirt during the finale of "Jumping Jack Flash," grabbed an American flag, and pranced offstage, where John H. White caught the weary Stone in a moment of lonely exhaustion.

She screams, she wails, she's disco queen Grace Jones (above), caught here at the Coop deVille, a New Haven disco where she caused temperatures to rise last winter. "She's a very kinky person," confides photographer Steve Silk, who adds that Ms. Jones dresses in animal skins and crawls through the audience.

121

Known for his television and toga antics, John Belushi (left) shows a more contemplative side during an interview at the Beverley Hills Hotel. "Out here some people are always 'on,'" says Tony Barnard, "but Belushi wasn't. He's really a little bit shy." For father-daughter duo Pat and Debbie Boone, the limelight is a lifestyle. Above, the clean crooner and Light Up My Life-er do a little cross-eyed clowning for the camera. At right, Steve Martin and his trusty banjo during a performance on the campus of the University of Missouri last spring. The collegiate cult hero had just finished a rendition of "Swanee" sung to the melody of "Ain't She Sweet." Enthuses Ed McCain, a devotee of many years' standing, "You never know what he's going to do next. He's completely illogical, but makes the absurd sound straight." What was that again?

SARAH E. LEEN, ARIZONA DAILY STAR (SECOND PLACE, PORTRAIT)

When Sarah Leen was assigned by her paper to cover a "media event" being staged at the Yacqui Indian village in Marana, Arizona, for the state's governor, she expected plenty of professional company—and encountered an army. Covering the village tour and handshaking ceremonies with tribal members were two television crews and reporters from three other papers. Deciding enough was enough, Leen began concentrating on the crowd—and discovered Ramona Sanchez (left) with young Julia Alverez, 11. Mrs. Sanchez, who does not quite remember how old she is, estimates her age at 103-105 years.

126

His badge draped in black, Robert Beasley (left), a member of the Arizona state livestock board, pays his respects to ex-Govenor Wesley Bolin, lying in state in the capitol retunda in Phoenix. Life is distinctly less somber for Jossie May Sims (above). While waiting for her best friend and cousin in the Georgetown, Mississippi post office, Jossie May pulls out a half-smoked cigar and lights up. She claims that cigars help clear her sinuses, and although she is kidded about her habit, she keeps on puffing. Whenever the mood strikes, there's Jossie May— and her stogie.

John Norton (right) lives in an all-male rooming house in Milwaukee's inner city, and when William Meyer came there on assignment, Norton caught his eye immediately. Taken aback by the spartan living conditions and depressing atmosphere, Meyer describes the assignment as a grim experience. "What struck me was that there was no interaction among the men," he recollects. "It was frightening."

SARAH E. LEEN, ARIZONA DAILY STAR

WILLIAM MEYER, MILWAUKEE JOURNAL

For roofer Raymond Gutierrez (above), laying tar in the heat of an Arizona summer is like working in a furnace. With sweat literally running off his body, Gutierrez lays four-hundred-degree tar on rooftops. "It's the hardest job I've ever had in my life," he declares.

128

For those who fear that the spirit of Abe Lincoln went out with log cabins, hope lives in Oregon. This family portrait, by Brian Lanker, of the children and grandchildren of former Oregon governor Bob Straub was taken while the clan was horse-logging on the governor's farm last summer. "Horse-logging went out many years ago," explains Lanker. "Few people do it nowadays and certainly not many governors' families." At left, Patty Straub Thomas, the ex-governor's twenty-nine-year-old daughter, is standing next to her husband, Jay, and her two sons, Moss, 6, and Sagebrush, 8. Standing next to Jay are Mike Straub, with his wife, Linna, and their five children. From left to right in the foreground, the brood of little Straubs and Thomases include Kathleen, Moss, Lana, Mary, Jimmer, Sagebrush and Michael. Says Patty, "You live in Oregon, you make the best of it."

130

DICK BELL, ST. PETERSBURG TIMES AND EVENING INDEPENDENT

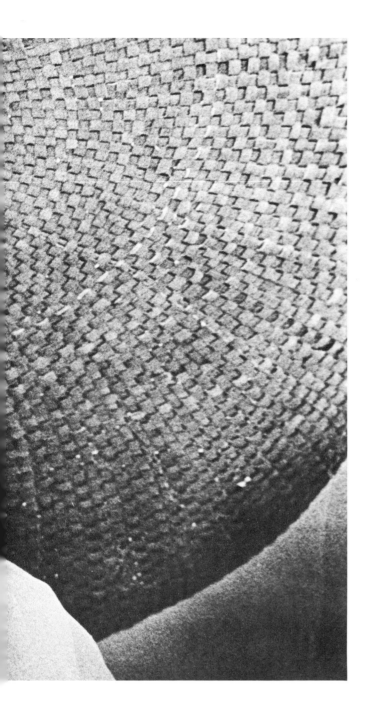

"She was so captivating, I just had to take her picture," says Dick Bell, who was covering an ethnic fair when he came across the little girl with the big eyes and the huge hat. Part of a group of recently-arrived immigrants from the Philippines, this shy little charmer—who spoke nary a word of English—was with her mother, who was dancing at a fair held at St. Petersburg Catholic High School. "The whole group was very excited about having their picture taken," declares Bell. "It seemed a big deal." Maybe not big enough, however, for although Bell's photograph appeared on the front page of his paper's local section, he never heard from his subjects.

Meet Tammy (near right), a seventeen-year-old with enough of a past to want to forget about it. Tammy's homemade tattoos are a part of the past she'd like to erase. "My feeling at the time was that she was a sweet girl who wanted to get rid of her tattoos," explains photographer Patty Reksten, who found Tammy while the girl was an inmate at the Missouri Training School for Girls at Chillicothe. Due for release from the school, Tammy said fervently, "I got to stay out of trouble."

"I wanted to capture his cocky attitude towards life, but also his sensitivity," explains Nick Kelsh, who shot the tattooed teenager (opposite), as part of a series on the Missouri Training School for Boys located in Boonville. This seventeen-year-old has been needling his skin since he was twelve. On the verge of release from the school, he is anxious to start a new life and obliterate these reminders of the past. "They look junky," he confesses.

PATTY REKSTEN, COLUMBIA (MISSOURI) DAILY TRIBUNE

134

NICK KELSH, COLUMBIA (MISSOURI) DAILY TRIBUNE (SECOND PLACE, FEATURE PICTURE STORY)

He's wanted to be a boxer since he was eight years old and he carries an article about Leon Spinks, the former world heavyweight champion, in his wallet. Yet at age sixteen, this inmate of the Boonville Training School for Boys has also been in jail three times and has a record that includes armed robberies, assaults, and purse snatchings. With the breezy confidence of a street-smart adolescent he says, "I can really make a go to be the greatest." Comments Nick Kelsh, who caught the budding boxer at Boonville, "He was really into boxing and I wanted to show that side of him, strong and powerful."

MITCH KEZAR, TAMPA TRIBUNE

Mitch Kezar describes his uncle, above, as "different," a seemingly accurate description of any man who yodels with pigs. Teck Kezar, 48, chose the pig in the picture when it was a mere piglet. Now that it has grown, he has come to fetch it. The pig has begun to squeal and Teck Kezar is doing the sensible thing— he's harmonizing.

High school honeys Becky Maples and Allan Gunthorp (right) were snuggling on the fence at the hog pavillion during the LaGrange County 4H Fair when Greg Dorsett caught squealers and sweethearts in mirror embraces. "I was in the right place at the right time," says Dorsett, "but I almost had a heart attack when I saw them."

By his own estimate, Al Zukosky's habit has cost him over $8,000 and taken up 4,000 - 5,000 hours spread over a twenty-six year period. "Some people are into golf, he's into tattoos," explains Skip Peterson, who came across Zukosky (near right) installing a printing press at Peterson's paper last summer. Stripped to the waist, Zukosky with his embellished epidermis caused even the most jaded journalists at the Dayton Daily News to take notice. Professing no preference for any particular needler, Zukosky's been tattooed in parlors across the U.S.—and he isn't finished yet: everything below his waist is untouched territory.

"She's everybody's favorite grandmother," declares Kent Kobersteen about the tattooed lady at far right. "She's a nifty little old lady who just happens to have pictures all over her body." Kobersteen came across Elizabeth Weinzirl, a great-grandmother from Portland, Oregon, at a Minneapolis tattoo parlor. (She was in town for a tattoo convention.) When she met Kobersteen, she naturally asked him if he would like to see her tattoos. With that, says Kobersteen, "she simply lifted her dress over her head and said, 'here they are.'" Mrs. Weinzirl, 76, later bared her all for Kobersteen at a local studio.

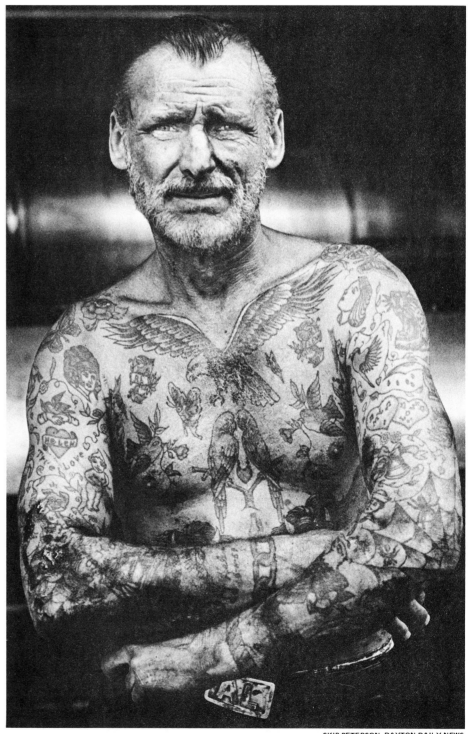

SKIP PETERSON, DAYTON DAILY NEWS

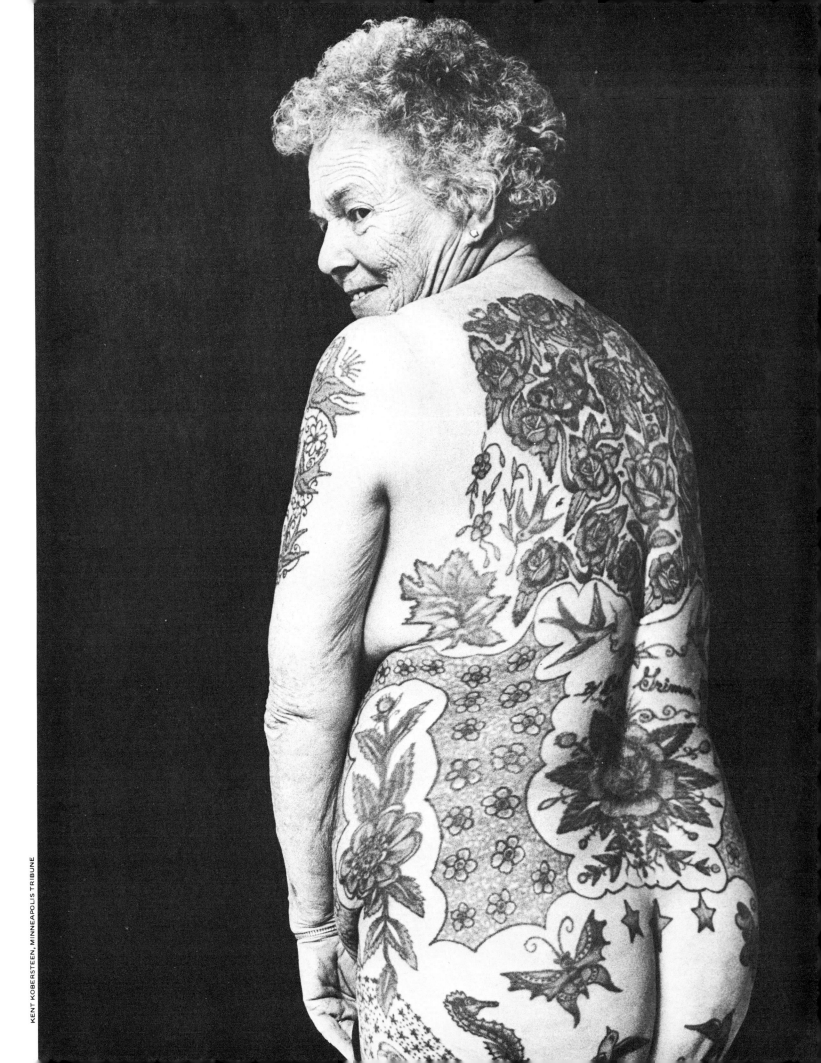

JOHN SHECKLER, (NEW BEDFORD, MASSACHUSETTS) STANDARD TIMES

Valentine's his name and hawking peanuts is his game. In Washington, D.C., no less. On vacation in the Capital City from the wilds of Colorado, Robert Tonsing was taking a leisurely drive past the Department of Justice when he caught Valentine's act. Valentine's buttons and badges are leftovers from '76, when he had a field day peddling Bicentennial baubles.

John Sheckler had just started working for his paper when he was assigned a story on dumps. Running late, he got to the city dump and immediately zeroed in on Alfred Silva (above), a part-timer who was helping people with their trash. Says Sheckler, "He struck me as one of the happiest people I have ever seen. He seemed to know everyone who came to the dump."

This man raises turkeys. Not only that, this man _loves_ turkeys. Since he was six years old, Tom Klopfenstein has been a turkey farmer, most recently at the Kaufman Ho-Ka Turkey Farm in Waterman, Illinois. "He's like a mother to them," declares John H. White, who shot the turkey maven in a sea of gobblers. Adds White: "I could see why he was so successful; he knew everything about them." And does the guardian of the gobblers ever eat his progeny? "He says he doesn't like them," shrugs White.

JOHN H. WHITE, CHICAGO SUN-TIMES

Down in Amish country, the mule and horse auction in New Holland, Pennsylvania, is not only a time for farmers to bargain for beasts but to shoot the breeze before the busy spring plowing season begins. "Instead of buying tires for the tractor, they buy a new set of mules," says Gene Puskar, who snapped these four gentlemen watching the bidding from the stands in front of a runway where mule teams were paraded. Puskar, who has covered the Amish for three and one-half years, says that he shot this genial group without their knowledge. "To them, posing for photographers is an act of vanity," says Puskar.

*Clareta Olmstead Smith is a
gentlewoman from a not-so-gentle
era. Delicately holding her
grandmother's fan, which dates
back to President Pierce's
inaugural, Miss Smith was
photographed by Jeffrey Hamilton
in the house she has lived in for
decades. The occasion was the
transfer of Olmstead Place to
the state of Washington.
Designated an historic landmark,
the nineteenth-century property
includes the family's original
log cabin and the farmhouse
where Miss Smith lives.*

*For most, Memorial Day means
picnics, beaches, and parties,
but for John Madsen, 81 (left),
and John Jones, 84, it is a day for
remembering. These two World
War I vets are among 585 former
soldiers who now live at the
Minnesota Veterans' Home in
south Minneapolis, which houses
men who fought in every war
from the Spanish-American
to the Vietnamese War. Last
May, the home had its annual
celebration—and Madsen
and Jones commemorated
Memorial Day in their own way.*

PHIL SCHERMEISTER, TOPEKA CAPITAL-JOURNAL

Her name is Hildegarde, and at 72 her hair is silky, her complexion flawless. After all, she's a doll. Stroking her blonde wig is her owner of the past seven decades, Mrs. Corinne Sayler of Topeka, Kansas, who received the porcelain beauty as a Christmas present in 1906. Says photographer Phil Schermeister of Mrs. Sayler: "She was sharp as a tack and remembered everything, especially about the doll. I felt she was very close to the doll because of all the memories, but realistic enough to see it as just a doll." No such memento exists for Thomas Smith (right), a former Missouri farmer who now lives a lonely life in a boardinghouse. He has only his thoughts and memories to help ease the pain of growing old alone.

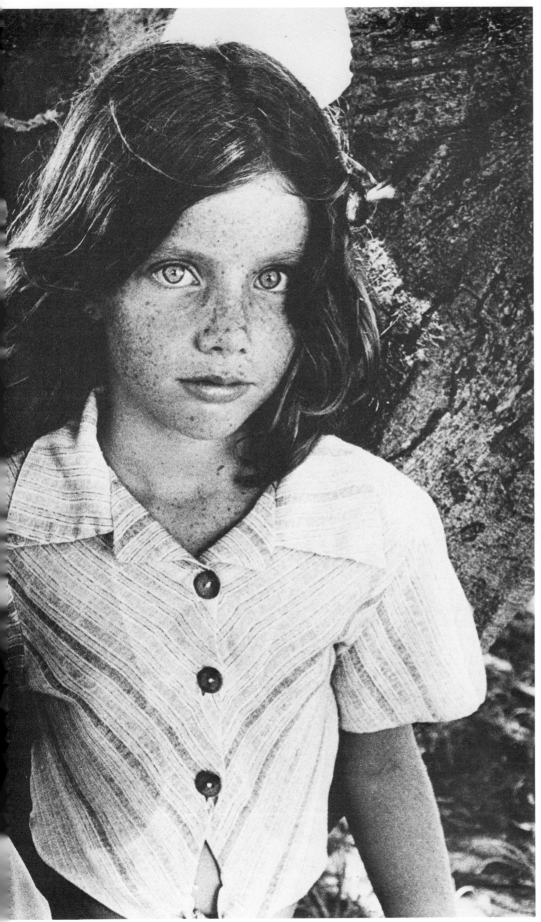

"Some siblings look alike and some siblings act alike," explains Keith Graham, who is making a photographic study of brothers and sisters. He came across the Hooper sisters last summer as (from left to right) Heather, 7, Cathy, 6, and Jackie, 8, were playing at Normandy Isle Park and Playground in North Miami Beach. "What struck me about them was that they looked so much alike," says Graham, adding, "I only wish there had been eight more just like them at home."

153

John White was late for another
assignment last spring when
he caught these human slinkies
in action in a vacant lot on
Chicago's West side. Stopping his
car, White took a series of shots
of the two flipping and springing.
Both thirteen-year-old Lezarrick
Davis (left) and twelve-year-old
Derick Larry (wearing cap)
told White they yearned to
become gymnasts; as a result
of White's photo-essay, they got
a coach. "Opening doors like
this is part of our job," says White.
"The camera is a passport, a
key; it can touch people in
a positive way. And it's a great
way of sharing."

JOHN H. WHITE, CHICAGO SUN-TIMES

155

WILLIAM J. LIZDAS, LACROSSE (WISCONSIN) TRIBUNE

DON B. STEVENSON, MESA (ARIZONA) TRIBUNE

At an age when most little girls are playing with dolls and sometimes boys, eleven-year-old Kim Neal (left) devotes six hours a day, seven days a week to gymnastics. A member of the Arizona Academy of Gymnasts and the state's hope for a spot on the U.S. Olympic Team, little Kim has already competed and placed in meets from New York to Japan. "Not bad for an eleven-year-old," quips Don Stevenson, who caught the pre-pubescent pretzel unawares as she was talking to her parents from the gym.

Taught to play an instrument without having learned to read music, these little violinists above (average age: four) gave a concert last April in the basketball court of the Racine, Wisconsin YWCA. William Lizdas waited over two hours to get this shot, which he feels "sums up the moment." It happened at a moment when the mini-musicians were supposed to raise their legs in time to the music (while still playing their instruments). Seems that the little girl at center lost the beat—much to her chagrin and Lizdas's delight.

The assignment was a little easier for Jebb Harris, who shot the budding ballerinas at right. Three-year-old Gretchen Antonini (in the dark tights) and Natalie Husband (with the blond hair) are students in a pre-school ballet class and when teacher Sonya Hensley demonstrated a body movement meant to relax, the toddlers responded by sticking their stomachs out—not exactly what Hensley had in mind. Says Harris, "Children are so loose and free, I just let them be the picture."

157

Some have called basketball, in its finer moments, a ballet— but in Chicago they've switched metaphors. This picture of Nana Solbrig, head of Chicago Ballet Theatre, was taken by Martha Harnett while the company was rehearsing for a half-time show at a Chicago Bulls game. Although this was not the effect she was aiming for, Harnett was quite pleased: "As a news photographer, I don't get to do this type of photo often," she says. "It's a nice change of pace." As for Solbrig—who is in her late thirties—Harnett says that "she is one of the most dynamic people I've ever met. At the age most people are slowing down, she has incredible energy." Small and wiry offstage, the dancer "fills the stage" once she's behind the footlights, according to Harnett.

Satisfaction has many faces. For the tired and happy shopper at left, standing in line to pay for a bundle of designer suits (slashed to half price during a one-day sale in Chicago) spells pleasure. For Paul Rachman (below), a semi-retired mannequin repairman who moved to Hollywood, Florida, from New York seven years ago, satisfaction comes from repairing and resurfacing the damaged Big Dolls. Working out of a garage in back of a house he uses as a storeroom, Rachman restores mannequins for local chain stores. Although his original ambition was to become an artist, Rachman has found contentment—and not a little pleasure—in his work. For butcher Tom Chaffer (opposite), who cleaves meat at the Rochester Public Market, no such artistic/professional schism exists. For Chaffer, slinging a pig over his shoulder with the panache of a star athlete is enough.

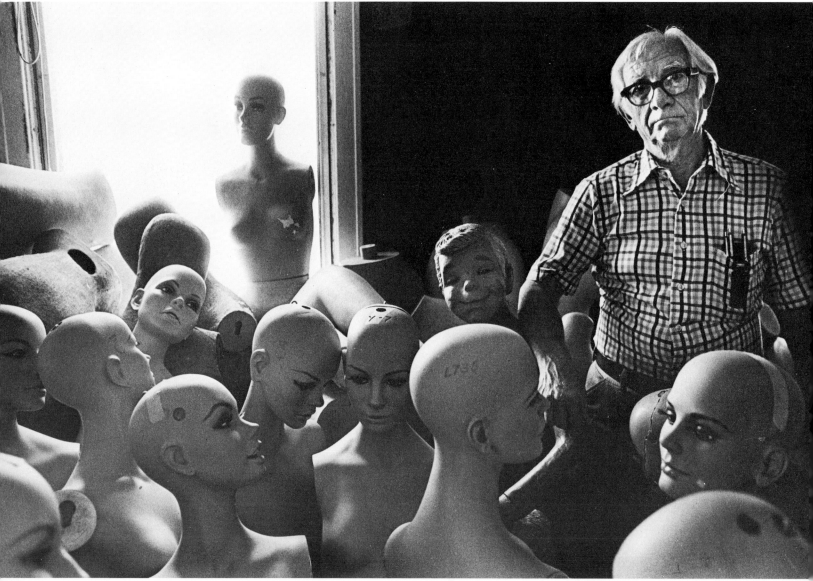

TALIS BERGMANIS, GANNETT/ROCHESTER NEWSPAPERS (SECOND PLACE, FOOD ILLUSTRATION)

How the camera can deceive. This seemingly bucolic scene below was really shot across a four-lane highway in Florida. Student Michael Diemer came across the young angler heading out to try his luck with bait *and rod. Another budding Florida fisherman (right) startled Murry Sill with his megawatt smile and button-bright eyes. Sill discovered Albert Jones in Hialeah, Florida, a Miami suburb.*

MICHAEL J. DIEMER, COLUMBIA MISSOURIAN

John H. White spotted the skateboard princess at lower right while on vacation in his native North Carolina. White, who did not find out very much about this particular young lady, admits to a special affection for kids. Having acquired his first camera fifteen years ago for fifty cents and ten gum wrappers, White tells kids, "I love gum too, but if you chew it you should read the labels."

162

*En route to cover a marathon
early one morning, Don Bartletti
saw this serene scene and reached
for his 500mm lens. Bartletti
later learned that the gentleman
reading his paper in the dawn's
early light is a seventy-one-year-
old retired Easterner who walks
five miles each day before settling
on this particular bench in this
San Diego park. Why this
bench? Seems that the sun
gets there before he does and
warms it up. Silly to ask.*

WORLD UNDERSTANDING AWARD

George Wedding

NO DEATH SEEMS so cruel, or proves so hard to reconcile, as the death that comes out of turn, defying the natural order of things and confounding our belief in Providence. Last year death took a beguiling nine-year-old Florida girl, Marguerita Beltran, out of turn — but not before she had waged a three-year battle, always valiantly, always futilely, with the malign force that had invaded her frail body. The Beltran family stood in helpless witness to little Marguerita's terrible ordeal month after month — and so did photographer George Wedding of the *Palm Beach Post-Times.* Wedding's grim chronicle of those years, winner of the 1978 Nikon World Understanding Award, begins with this charming candid of what he describes as a "deceptively healthy-looking" Marguerita. Photographer Wedding took this particular picture in early September of 1976, by which time Marguerita was already subject to the recurrent spells of profound dizziness and the headaches that had led the young girl's doctors to diagnose her inoperable brain tumor. Their chilling and accurate prognosis: "Three years at the most."

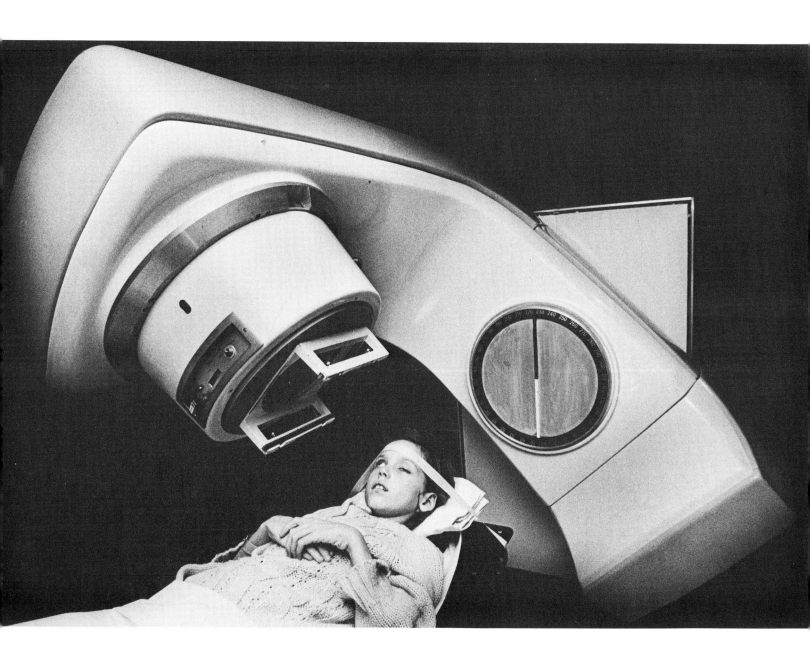

"I understand God tests us by seeing how much we can bear," Marguerita Beltran's mother said to photographer Wedding at one point—adding, after a long pause, "but sometimes I just don't think I can bear any more." There was much to endure during the three-year course of little Marguerita's illness, and the Beltran family shared the burden as best they could. For the afflicted girl herself there was radiation therapy (above), which the doctors hoped would shrink her inoperable tumor. As Wedding notes, these sessions eventually became routine, but being strapped down beneath the sinisterly elegant apparatus never lost its terror. For the stoic, steadfast Earline Beltran there were countless trips to hospitals in Miami and West Palm Beach, Florida, in search of some respite, however temporary, for the youngest of her eleven children. And there were the endless vigils (left) over a daughter too wasted by disease and too debilitated by therapy to walk or even talk.

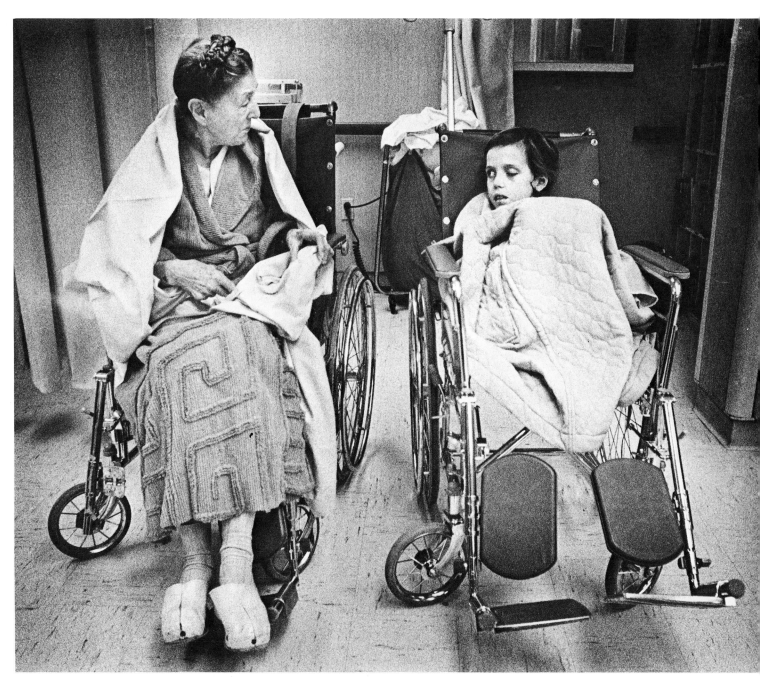

It is often said of cancer that it is a disease which engenders hope. First, of course, you hope you don't actually have cancer. Then you hope you will be cured. Then you hope for a reprieve—a year or two, another birthday, a final Christmas. Towards the end you find yourself hoping for simpler things—a good day, a pain-free night, an easy rest. In the photograph at right, Marguerita finds such momentary solace in her mother's encircling arms and constant grip. (Inked lines in front of Marguerita's left ear served to guide the radiotherapist.) At left, a listless Marguerita listens to 81-year-old Mercedes Taylor, herself the victim of a brain tumor. For Mercedes, at the other end of life, the need for hope is not nearly so great, and the prospect of an easy rest is nearer at hand.

After two years of radiation treatments and chemotherapy, a bedridden Marguerita Beltran bears little resemblance to the beaming, bright-eyed girl whom George Wedding first photographed in September, 1976. This transformation is strikingly apparent in the picture at left, for Wedding's original portrait can be seen hanging above the sick girl's bed, a grim memento vitae. Wan and reed-thin, she lies in a hospital bed that has been installed at home. (Her left eye is, by now, forced closed by the tumor growing behind it.) At right, Marguerita's stepfather takes her out for an airing—a gesture that would prove increasingly ineffectual as her condition deteriorated.

Classmates and relatives gather on the front lawn on March 25, 1978, to help Marguerita celebrate her ninth—and last—birthday. A ruffled bonnet conceals the extent of her hair loss, a side effect of the radiation therapy.

OVERLEAF: As word of Marguerita's plight began to reach the wider world—in large part through Wedding's poignant photo-essays—gifts begin to arrive from strangers touched by her tale. At first Marguerita's mother hung these dolls and plush toys on the wall over her daughter's bed, but she took them all down when Marguerita lapsed into a coma.

As commonly happens with such treatment, massive irradiation of Marguerita's tumor proved initially efficacious. This was, as it turned out, nothing more than a landing on a descending staircase—the cruel illusion of remission, not remission itself—but for a time she actually gained weight and strength. Most of the rest of her hair fell out, leaving only a soft nimbus of fuzz, but her left eye reopened—a sign the tumor lodged just behind it had in fact been reduced in size.

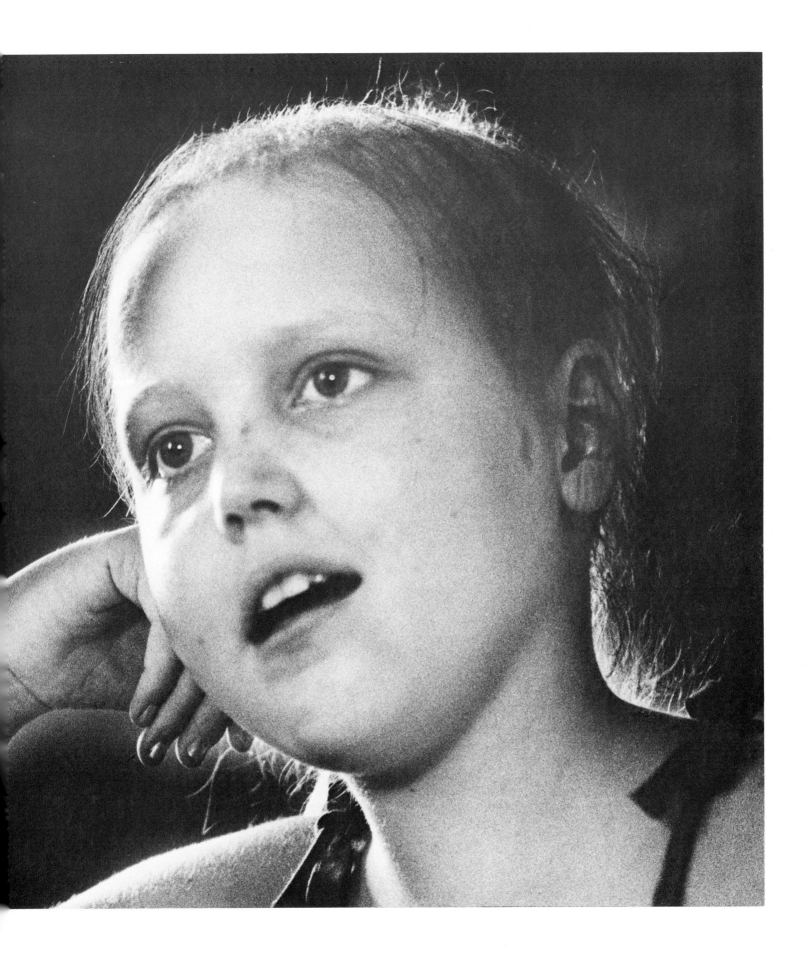

The last vigil began on New Year's Eve, 1979. Marguerita had lapsed into a coma earlier in the day, and the family had taken her to the hospital, as they had done so many times in the past. This time, however, the doctors told her mother and stepfather that there was nothing more medicine could do for Marguerita—and she came home for the last time.

The family sat in shifts at her bedside—sister Oma is seen below—as the little girl's breathing became shallower and more labored, and on the sixth day Reverend Clifford Kilgore was summoned. At far right he checks Marguerita's pulse, which came at last to easy rest at 11:45 A.M. on Friday, January 5.

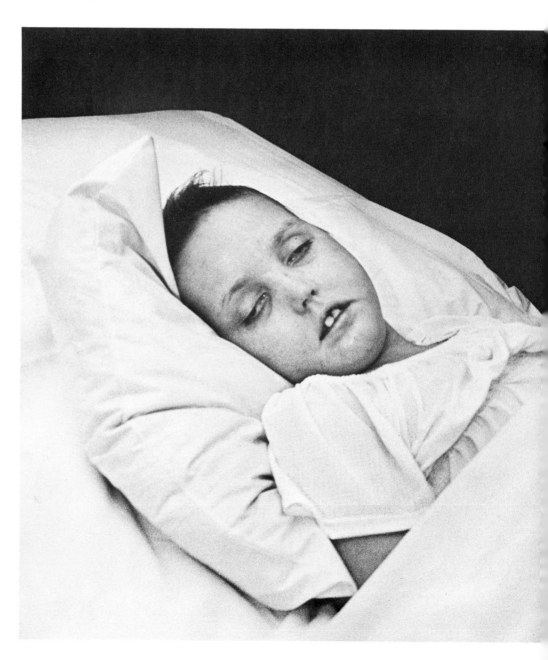

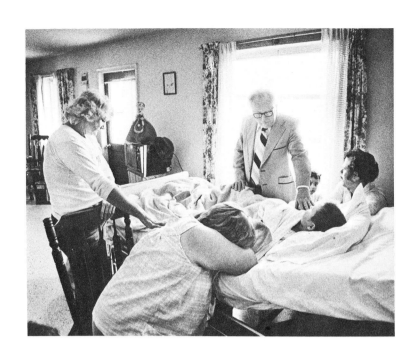

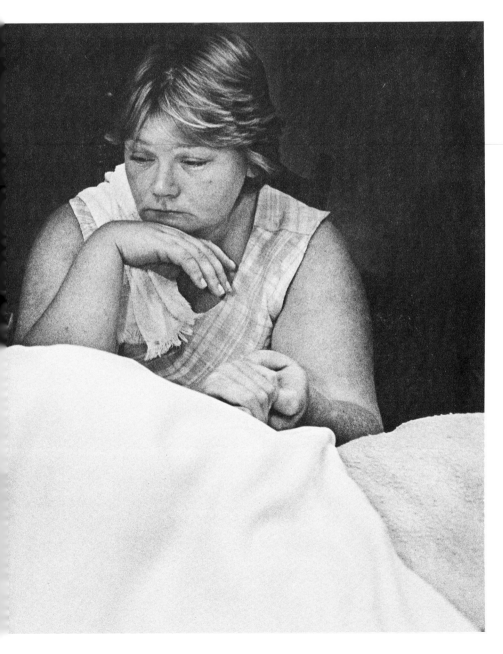

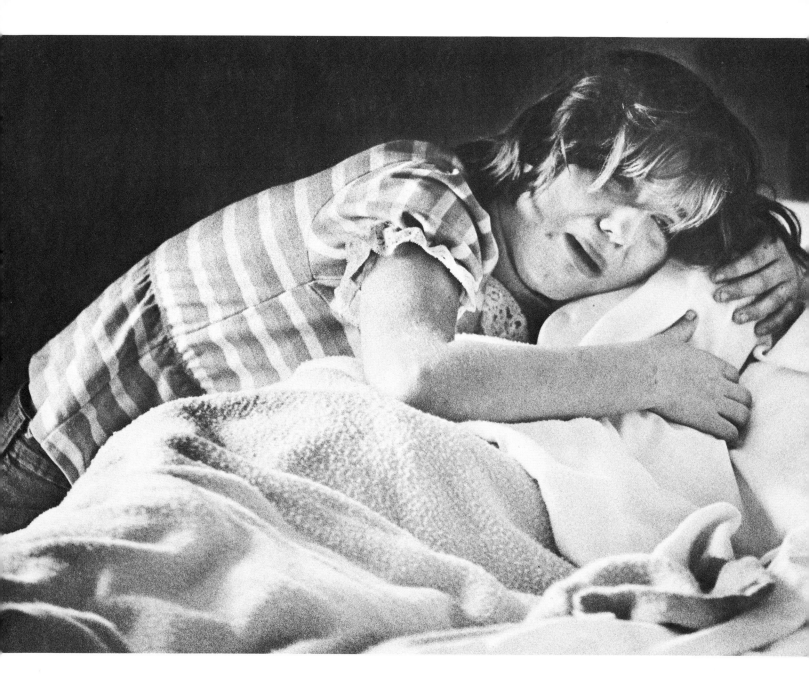

After three long years of hoping against hope, Marguerita's family at last found itself confronting hope's end, the harsh reality of death itself. Carol (left), who was so close to Marguerita in age and who shared so much of the ordeal firsthand, found it all but impossible to accept the idea that her sister had actually died, and she insisted upon giving Marguerita's lifeless body a final embrace. At the little girl's funeral (below), the satin casket-lining and all the flowers were white—and all the hymns were personal favorites.

FEATURE STORIES

THE CAMERA can transcend the political, geographic, and linguistic barriers that might otherwise thwart our attempts to achieve some understanding of other cultures — and we owe much of what we know about distant lands and their peoples to the work of the photographers represented in this section. Feature stories may lack the immediacy of hard news, but they more than compensate in terms of human interest. And that, in the end, may be the more durable quality. Take James L. Stanfield's photo-essay on Syria, for instance: it focuses not on that country's crucial role in Levantine politics but on its people. The first consideration may be timely, but the second is timeless. "In some villages," *National Geographic* photographer Stanfield reports, "life has changed very little since the time of Christ." In the tiny settlement of Tel Mardikh, for instance, where photographer Stanfield came upon this angelic three-year-old and her wizened grandmother, villagers still speak Aramaic, the language used two millennia ago by Jesus of Nazareth and his disciples, and women still dress in Biblical garb.

In the words of photographer
James L. Stanfield, the history
of modern Syria is a "chronicle
of chaos": in the first twenty-
four years of the nation's
existence its central government
has changed twenty-three times,
Political turmoil in Damascus
has had little impact on life in
the tiny northern village of
Tel Mardikh, however. There
the overwhelming sense is one
of continuity, not chaos; little
has changed since Biblical times.
Families still share quarters in
the sun-reddened, mud-brick
compound at left, whose beehive
roofs cover living spaces and
a communal granary. And
sheepherding Bedouins—among
them Muhammad Diab and his
tattooed wife, above—still tend
flocks on the Syrian littoral,
much as their ancestors did in
the days of the Crusaders, when
Syria was known as Outremer,
the land beyond the sea.
Stanfield's double portrait
captures an intimacy the Bedouin
rarely reveal to strangers.

187

The very incarnation of an Old Testament prophet, Najib al-Hamoud (far left) is an elder of the Druze sect, whose holy mountain, Jabal ad Duruz, rises high above Syria's southern plain not far from the Jordanian border. Time and the vagaries of war have scattered the sect, and Druze enclaves are now found in Lebanon and even Israel. A number of these descendants of ancient nomads are blond-haired and blue-eyed—the result, elders say, of intermarriage between the Druzes and Alexander the Great's soldiers.

"The eye also feasts," the Syrians are fond of saying, and their eye-dazzling suqs, or open-air bazaars, are famous the world over. "Atchan, taa saubi!—If you thirst, come to me!"—sellers cry—and Afghans and Turks, Sudanese and Pakistanis, Iraqis and Kurds respond to their call. For the moment it is only the eye that feasts below, however. The grocer has paused to brush his teeth in the trickle of water that flows past his front door, and his customer of the moment, a Catholic priest, is obliged to wait.

One woman, young and adventurous; one dog, loyal and wily; four camels, feral and recalcitrant; and 1,700 miles of Australian outback, sere and forbidding. Substitute a man, preferably a middle-aged Englishman, for the young woman and you have the elements of a classic nineteenth-century adventure saga. But this is the twentieth century, and so our protagonist is a woman, dreaming what was once thought of as a man's dream: a solo trek across western Australia's two deserts, the Great Sandy and the Gibson. After two years of preparation, Robyn Davidson set out from a point just east of Ayer's Rock (right), the striking geological formation that is the region's most famous landmark. Her half-year odyssey took its toll on the camels, who needed constant nursing and comforting (left) en route to the Indian Ocean (above).

Photographer Thomas J. Abercrombie calls Ladakh, India's most remote province, "the last Shangri-la"—and the sobriquet certainly seems to fit. If there is any spot on the globe where the ills of modern society do not seem to impinge, it is here in this Himalayan fastness (below), which shares common borders with Tibet, China, and Pakistan.

The arid uplands and glacier-fed streams of Ladakh support a populace of roughly 200,000, half of them Buddhists and half Moslems. Of these, 15,000 live in the principal city of Leh, once an important stop on central Asia's fabled caravan routes. In those days wool from Tibet and silks from China passed through Leh. Now, of course, those borders are closed and the strangers who pass through Leh are mostly Indian troops, 40,000 of whom are charged with garrisoning Ladakh's frontiers. In good times and bad, the cornerstones of Ladakhi culture have been its gompas, or "solitary places," among them the lamasery at Lamayuru (left), which seems to grow straight out of the rock face upon which it sits.

The Ladakhis, a profoundly religious people, celebrate the birthday of Padma Sambhaya, the eighth-century founder of Tibetan Buddhism, with a June festival (below). But worship is not confined to festival periods, as the double portrait at left indicates. These elderly men carry burnished copper prayer wheels, in the belief that each turn of the scripture-filled wheel sends fresh supplications heavenward.

The amulets and needles festooning the wool cap of the toddler above are intended to ward off evil spirits. What they cannot ward off, though, are the unwelcome advances of a foreign photographer. No such timidity is seen at left, where a beaming government worker poses in an elaborate headdress of rough-cut turquoises.

OVERLEAF: Ground fog lay dense about the reconstructed ramparts of Fort George when photographer Sam Abell arrived on assignment. The result looks remarkably like a Hudson River School landscape.

ALL: THOMAS J. ABERCROMBIE, NATIONAL GEOGRAPHIC

197

Even in an age of superlatives, it was a catastrophe without precedent: the supertanker <u>Amoco</u> <u>Cadiz</u> lost her steering as she entered the English Channel, and after twelve hours of rudderless drifting—and three failed rescue attempts—she went aground (above) on rocky shoals off the coast of Brittany. "The bow was twisting and heaving in front of us," recollects one crew member—and then the ship's back broke, dumping 69 <u>million</u> gallons of oil into the sea (right). The resultant spill threatened to bury Brittany's thriving fishing industry more or less permanently under a thick layer of black, viscous, life-stifling goo (left).

ALL: MARTIN ROGERS, NATIONAL GEOGRAPHIC (FIRST PLACE, NEWS PICTURE STORY/MAG AND HONORABLE MENTION, NEWS/MAG)

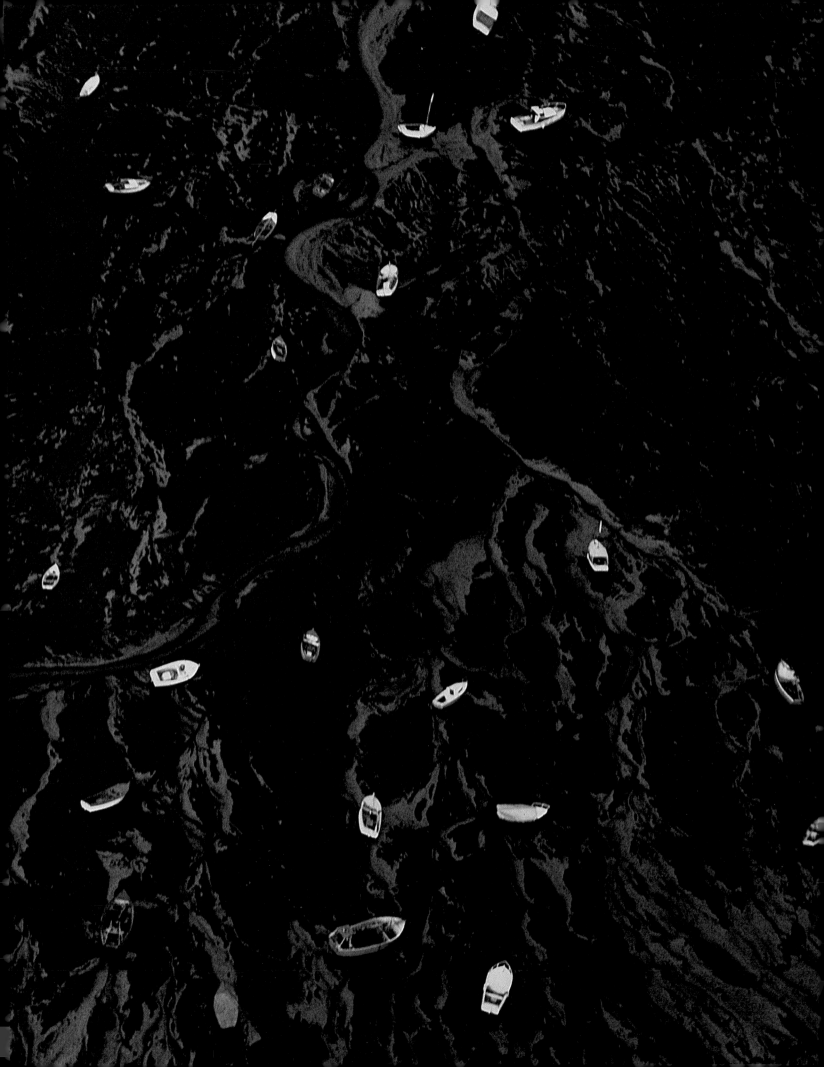

"_La mer est morte_—the sea is dead," cried anguished Bretons as they surveyed their suffocated shores, awash in Arab oil. And for weeks after the accident it seemed quite possible that the inky fluid leaking from the sundered hull of the _Amoco Cadiz_ would extinguish most of the marine life along some 100 miles of the Brittany coast. To combat the spill, army details and regiments of volunteers joined forces (above) to swab the beaches and sop up the encroaching slime. Using whatever implements they could lay their hands on, including brooms and shovels (right), men struggled to turn back the russet tide. While the Breton fishing fleet rode at anchor in a chocolate sea (left), experts debated the possible impact of the spill on the region's multimillion-dollar seaweed-chemical industry and, more importantly, on the fishing banks and oyster beds that had once provided France with one-third of its seafood.

ALL: MARTIN ROGERS, NATIONAL GEOGRAPHIC (FIRST PLACE, NEWS PICTURE STORY/MAG AND HONORABLE MENTION, NEWS/MAG)

In the glory days of vaudeville, performers identified two very separate show circuits, known universally as Big Time and Small Time. Big Time was the so-called Orpheum circuit—headlining, week-long runs in legendary houses like the Palace in New York City. Small Time was bottom-of-the-ticket, one-night stands in ill-lit and unheated municipal auditoriums across the American heartland. The circus also has a Big Time and a Small Time— and lion-tamer Larry Grant

(top) is part of the latter. His charges leap as nimbly (opposite) and nuzzle as menacingly (above) as any others, but the Circus Vargas, to which they all belong, does not play Madison Square Garden, which is circus Big Time. It plays shopping center parking lots in countless small towns, and consequently Grant and his great cats are often obliged to create their special magic for half-empty houses—and then to while away the hours (near left) between one show and another.

ALL: RICH FRISHMAN, THE EVERETT (WASHINGTON) HERALD

First woman miner forced to quit-- 40 Years Ago

No females in local mines -- yet

She has the look of so many older mountain women—the seamed face, the gnarled fingers, and the shining eyes—but Ida Mae Stull (left) is no ordinary mountain woman. Age and infirmity have slowed her down, and her once-brisk gait is now a bit tentative (above), but forty years ago she was a force to be reckoned with in the Ohio hills she has always called home. The 1930's were the years of John L. Lewis and "Bloody Harlan," of the bitter

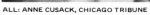

ALL: ANNE CUSACK, CHICAGO TRIBUNE

struggle to unionize the coal industry, and Ida Mae was a part of that struggle—not as a miner's wife but as one of a handful of female colliers working at what had traditionally been regarded as an exclusively male occupation. And when Ida Mae lost her job, simply because she was a woman, she took her case to court—and won. Harrison County, Ohio, may not remember Ida Mae's victory, but the memory sustains her in her retirement.

ALL: MIMI FULLER, CINCINNATI POST

To balletomanes, Christmas is "The Nutcracker," that perennial favorite—as the ad copy has it— of children of all ages. What theatergoers see is an airy illusion: a Christmas tree that grows onstage, and toys that come to life...Snowflakes and a Sugar Plum Fairy that seem to float above the boards, wafted along by Tchaikowsky's delightful score. What the theatergoer doesn't see is the endless effort and tireless professionalism which produce that illusion. For the dancers, Christmas is leg-warmers and limbering exercises and worn-out toe-shoes—and it is this aspect of the art of illusion that photographer Mimi Fuller has captured here.

The story is an old one: only the place and the players have changed. This time the locale is Quebec, not the Great Plains, and the red men are Crees, not Sioux—residents of a small island in Hudson Bay. The white men are not trappers or settlers but civil engineers who are constructing a hydroelectric plant that will eventually submerge the Indian settlement. When that day comes the rising waters will obliterate a way of life that has already been inundated by an alien culture—one that has replaced tepees with mobile homes, skins with denim, and tribal totems with Christian hymnals.

Two things distinguish the
Buckman farm in northern Ohio
from other, equally prosperous
working farms in the region. The
first is that the five men who
work the 150-acre spread are
brothers, ranging in age from 56
to 66. The second is that three
of the five are deaf-mutes.
Lined up at right for a group
portrait are, from left: Henry,
Carl, Ralph, George and Albert.

Because they understand each other far better than the world understands them, the Buckman brothers have never separated; they live and work together just as they have done for half a century, communicating by sign language. "I think God wanted it this way," observes their sister Mary, "so we could all take care of the deaf brothers." Care they clearly do, not only for each other but for their farm, which occupies them from sunup to well after sundown.

BILL BALLENBERG, GLOUCESTER (NEW JERSEY) COUNTY TIMES

We often liken the calendar year to a human life span—the diapered New Year giving way to that stooped graybeard, Father Time. Reckoned in like fashion, the date on which these pictures were taken is December 31 in the life of Fred Leigh, an 89-year-old retired glass maker from Clayton, New Jersey. Bill Ballenberg dubbed his studies of Leigh "The Winter of His Years," for he sensed that the old man had reached the end of his skein of days. Sapped of energy—and, with it, of his enthusiasm for living—Leigh still made ineffectual attempts to trim his stubble with a superannuated shaver (far left, below), and he spent some part of each day sitting on the porch of his weather-beaten house (near left). But he spent increasingly long stretches of time lying on the daybed in his living room (below), bundled against the cold his body could no longer dispel. And on the day before Ballenberg's story was published, he died.

SPORTS

IT IS IN THE ARENA of sports photography that we encounter the wildest extremes of emotion, from unbridled elation to unfathomable despair. "The agony of defeat" is only a phrase, and a hackneyed one at that, until it attaches itself to a photograph as powerful as the one opposite. Lensman Jerry Lodriguss zeroed in on boxer Victor Galindez moments after challenger Mike Rossman stripped him of his title, and Lodriguss' close-up of the ex-champ's battered and bloodied profile says more about defeat than mere words ever could. Eloquence is only one aspect of sports photography, however; elegance is another, as James Sugar's gull's-eye view of a catamaran race and surf-drenched close-up of windsurfing (pages 226-27) readily attest. And there is something else: a sense of mood, of the magic in a particular moment, that is evoked through a combination of the two. This combination can produce very successful, very dissimilar results from the same basic material, as the two uncommon photographs of an altogether common subject — football — on pages 228-29 confirm.

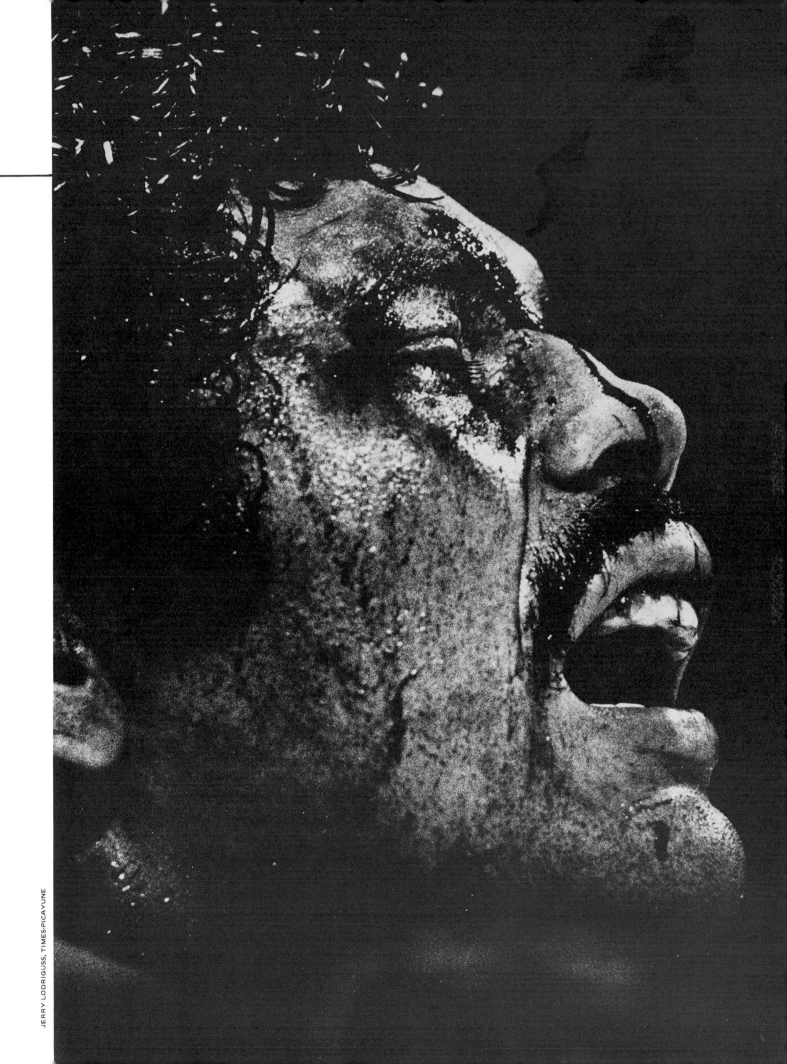

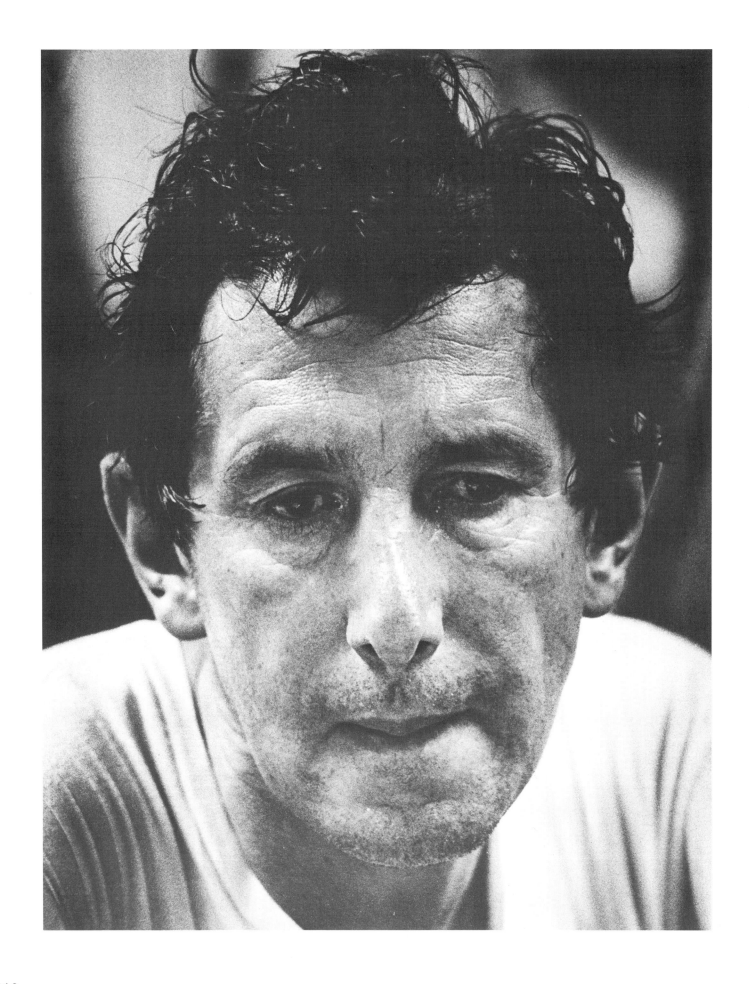

There's something about the pace of baseball that makes us think of hot, languid summer afternoons— when what we should be thinking of is hot tempers and quick-to-rile natures. Last year the Yankees were hot—in every sense of the word—and the team made as much news off the field as on it. In the most celebrated of many clashes between supercoach and superstar, Billy Martin (left) suspended Reggie Jackson (below) for disobeying Martin's order to hit—not bunt—during a game with the Kansas City Royals.

In a more innocent time, when adolescent males actually worried about having impure thoughts, one formula for banishing an unwanted erotic thought was to repeat the word "baseball" over and over. One wonders what our unflappable ump is thinking as Chicago Cubs manager Herman Franks scuffs the dust around him. "Raquel, Raquel," perhaps?

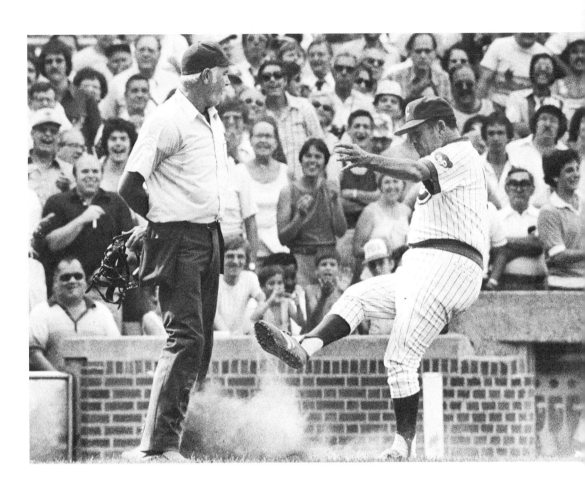

ALL: PHIL MASCIONE, CHICAGO TRIBUNE

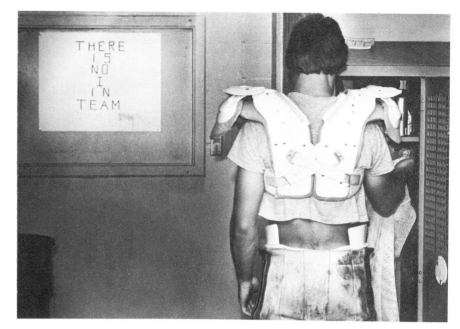

It's no wonder that American men feel almost universally nostalgic about their high school years. Never again in life will the pressures be as few, the structure as simple, the goals as immediate, the rewards as tangible, or the fruits of victory as sweet. Self-doubt and ambivalence, reversals and resignation—these are future concerns, if they are concerns at

ALL: ALEX BURROWS, CINCINNATI ENQUIRER (FIRST PLACE, SPORTS PICTURE STORY)

all; the present is sure and secure. For high school senior George Rudd, All-American and team player, the nostalgia is already settling in as the school year ends. His victories are all behind him, and he can only guess what lies ahead. He has his trophies, his teammates, and his girl (lower right)...but perhaps even she belongs more to his past than to his future.

Not crew members of the starship Enterprise, sleeping away the light-years of a mission into deep space, but members of the University of Oregon's swimming team, who begin each workout with a half-hour session of group hypnosis. Their coach, who initiated this exotic variation on the standard warm-up drill, insists that he can get his charges to levitate their hands on command by the session's end. Whether he can achieve the same sort of response in the pool is open to speculation. The merman at far right, en route to victory in a 400-meter freestyle event, looks less hypnotized than galvanized—by the desire to win.

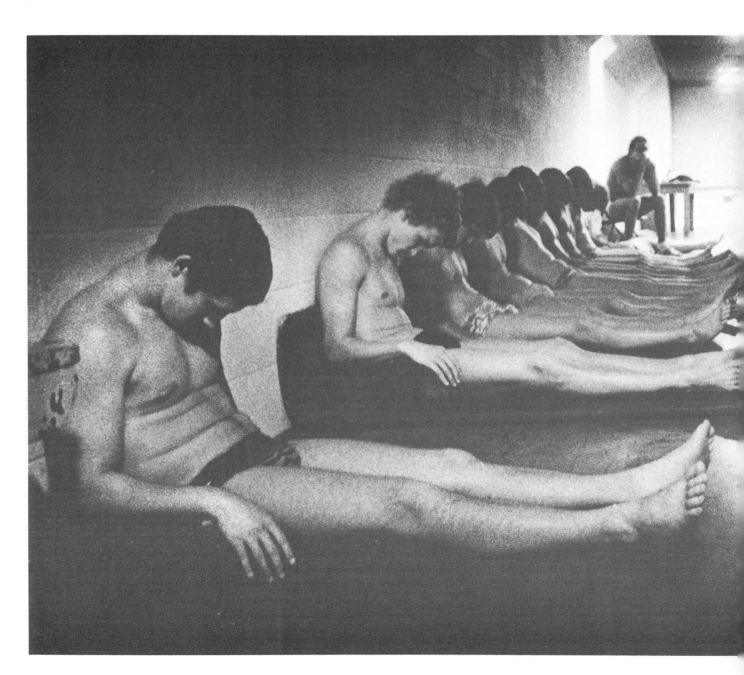

TOM KENNEDY, GAINESVILLE SUN

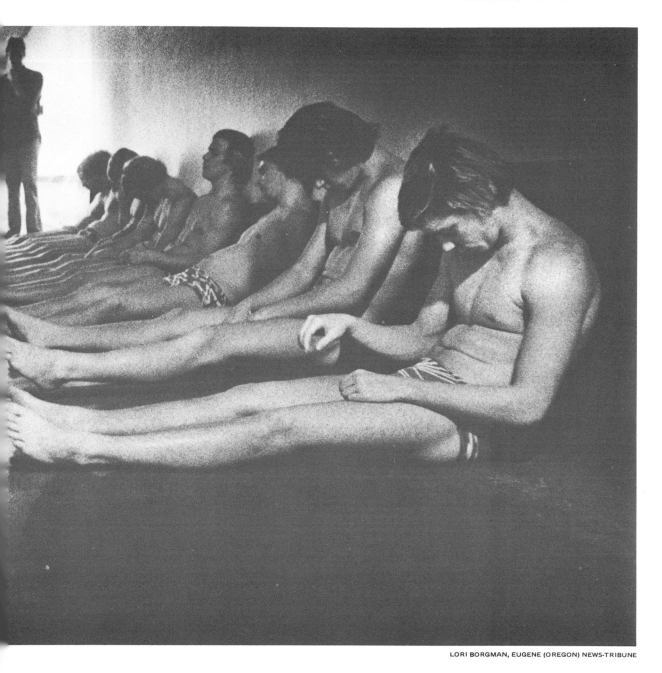

LORI BORGMAN, EUGENE (OREGON) NEWS-TRIBUNE

The long, level—and, on this
particular Sunday, carless—sweep
of the Verrazano-Narrows Bridge
(left) has always seemed a fitting
place for the New York City
Marathon to begin. But from 100
feet up on one of the bridge's
suspension towers, the double
band of concrete looks more like
a marble-chute than a racetrack.

Perhaps the rain gods are also
distance runners, for they chose
to favor Atlanta, Georgia, with
this summer cloudburst just
as the overheated participants
in last year's Peachtree Marathon
were crossing the finish line.

OVERLEAF: Two of James
Sugar's elegant compositions:
at the left, a windsurfer—part
wind, part surfer, part surf; at
right, a convocation of sleek
catamarans—blade-like hulls
and great bellying sails.

CHUCK ROGERS, BLACK STAR, ORIGINAL IN COLOR

227

*The subject, of course, is football.
The college team at left is the
Georgia Bulldogs, knees bent in
a moment of pre-game prayer. The
high school team above is from
Kansas, and as their jubilant
gestures indicate, a driving rain
has not kept them from a
state championship.*

The arm is cocked, the ball is released, and from that point on the quarterback and the opposing team members are mere spectators: the action is downfield. In this instance the quarterback is Craig Morton of the Denver Broncos (second from right)—and the action is an interception during the first quarter of the twelfth annual Super Bowl.

During the course of a race the eyes may wander—to the scoreboard, to the exit, to a head of especially luxuriant blond hair. But at the finish all eyes are on the tape, none more so, naturally, than the timekeepers'. These fixed gazes— and decidedly mixed reactions— were recorded by photographer Jim Jennings at a track meet in Richmond, Virginia.

The POY judges found both these shots of the sport of kings worthy of citation, perhaps because they capture two very fundamental— and fundamentally different— aspects of the same sport: the grace, and the peril. David Boyer's view (left) suggests a Kline canvas, so abstract are the forms, so bold the break-up of space into lights and darks. Melissa Farlow's subject (right) is a steeplechase mishap, one that poses an equal threat to rider and riderless mount.

MELISSA FARLOW, COURIER-JOURNAL AND LOUISVILLE TIMES (THIRD PLACE, SPORTS ACTION)

Hard to tell if it's subtext or simply coincidence, but <u>Los Angeles</u> <u>Times</u> lensman Andy Hayt seems to have an especially elastic preception of professional athletes. In one case the stretch is up, up, and away; in the other it's strictly earthbound... but in both instances the intent is to defy nature, to overreach the possible. For ebullient Dwight Stone (above), intent proved insufficient: he failed in this attempt to establish a new high-jump record. When Kareem Abdul-Jabbar (far right) breaks records, he does so by standing up and reaching upward. The knee-bends are just part of his warm-up.

In the 1600's there was no such thing as football—or baseball, or basketball, or soccer, or even cricket. There was a primitive form of rugby, just as there was pelota in the Americas, but we do not play those games today. What the seventeenth century did produce was The Compleat Angler, Izaak Walton's timeless treatise on the joys of fishing. What Walton was doing, more than three centuries ago, was codifying something his contemporaries already knew, namely that fishing—for sport, rather than provender—was not only the oldest but also the most contemplative and pleasurable of outdoor leisure activities. Crystalline waters, a well-caulked canoe, a dozen hand-tied flies, a certain crisp authority in the breeze...and the day is made. The right equipment, the right technique, the right hour— and some luck—may yield a creel of Brownies (near left) at day's end, but it's only the incompleat angler who needs a catch to justify his colloquy with nature.

DAVID PETERSON, DES MOINES REGISTER

It's the stuff movies used to be
made of: six times the soccer
team at right reaches the playoffs
for the state championship, and
six times they're defeated. On
the seventh try they battle their
way to a tie—and are forced
into a sudden-death overtime.
Final reel: the blond in the
foreground, assisted by
the two exultant teammates
behind him, boots in the winning
goal—and six years of almost-
but-not-quite are revenged.
Rugby is soccer with the gloves
off, the very definition of a
"man's sport." Except that all
of the ruggers seen above
happen to be female.

J. PAT CARTER, THE BALTIMORE SUNPAPERS

A survey of Third World nations once identified him as the most admired man in the world—both better known and more highly respected than any chief of state, including his own President. But life can be lonely at the top, especially when the object of admiration is no longer young and no longer heavyweight champion of the world. Sequestered at his training camp outside Deer Park, Pennyslvania, a 37-year-old Muhammad Ali prepares for his upcoming bout with Leon Spinks. "I have to win this fight," the ex-champion declares with fervor. "Too many people will be hurt if I lose."

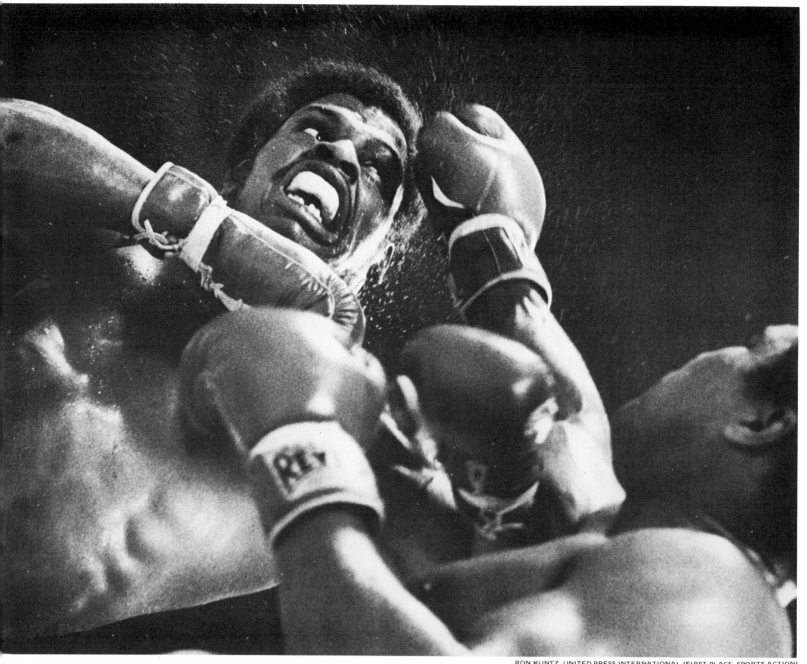

RON KUNTZ, UNITED PRESS INTERNATIONAL (FIRST PLACE, SPORTS ACTION)

KEITH WILLIAMS, COURIER-JOURNAL AND LOUISVILLE TIMES

For Muhammad Ali, victory would mean capturing the heavyweight crown for an unprecedented third time, but win or lose, his place in boxing annals—and sports fans' hearts— was already secure. Leon Spinks, on the other hand, had come from nowhere to strip Ali of his title, and defeat for him could well mean a long backward slide down the slippery slope he had so recently ascended. As it turned out, the man with the most to lose won—and Spinks responded with a triumphal roar (below) that seemed to lift him above the circle of his admirers, to give him the stature men have associated with the victorious warrior throughout human history.

GARY ANGELL, UNITED PRESS INTERNATIONAL (THIRD PLACE, SPORTS FEATURE)

Rain is only a handicap if you have no others. It temporarily cools the hot bat of Rod Carew at left, but the interruption is passing, the talent secure. For Robert Trotter, right, the interruption—which was polio and occurred when he was nine—is permanent, but it has not interfered with Trotter's athletic career. At 23, he is the player-coach of the Chicago Pacemakers, a wheelchair basketball team that competes nationally.

JOHN H. WHITE, CHICAGO SUN-TIMES (HONORABLE MENTION, FEATURE PICTURE STORY)

ZACK RYALL, AUSTIN (TEXAS) AMERICAN-STATESMAN

*To alleviate the tedium of the
workout sessions—and, not
incidentally, to spur themselves
to greater prodigies of lifting—
serious bodybuilders generally
work out with a regular training
partner. In the case above, the
goggle eyes and drooping facial
hair belong to an aspirant to
the title of Mr. Texas; the blond
frieze and distended veins to
his training partner. To alleviate
the tedium of prison life—and,
not incidentally, to establish
a tough reputation within the
prison's hierarchy—many inmates
take up weightlifting. Bryan
Grigsby found this menacing
exponent of the sport in a state
penitentiary in Florida.*

BRYAN K. GRIGSBY, GAINESVILLE SUN

OVERLEAF: *A significant part of growing up is simply perfecting the art of imitating adults— without looking any sillier than they do. In this as in all other things, practice makes perfect. And although these Little League players have the outward form down pat, they still need work on the substance of "Gimme Five."*

REX D. LARSEN, THE GRAND RAPIDS (MICHIGAN) PRESS

249

BRUCE H. BISPING, MINNEAPOLIS TRIBUNE

250

Minnesota is legendary for three things: its lakes, its forests, and its winters. And Minnesotans are legendary for three things: their intense enthusiasm for ice-fishing (what else do you do with all those lakes during all that winter?); their rabid loyalty to their professional football team, the Vikings; and their boundless bonhomie in the face of sub-zero temperatures and chest-high drifts. Minnesotans talk ice-fishing the way Californians talk tennis; the Vikings the way New Yorkers talked baseball during the days of the Subway Series; and wind-chill factors the way brokers talk Dow-Jones closing averages. Oddly enough, the two men at left aren't talking. Perhaps they will perk up when the Vikings hit the field. At right, a stadium in a sunnier clime: Arizona. In at least one respect the outcome of every game held here can be predicted in advance: whatever the score, the fans will leave behind some five and a half _tons_ of trash, including an estimated 10,000 bottles, ranging in size from one-ounce miniatures to one-gallon jugs.

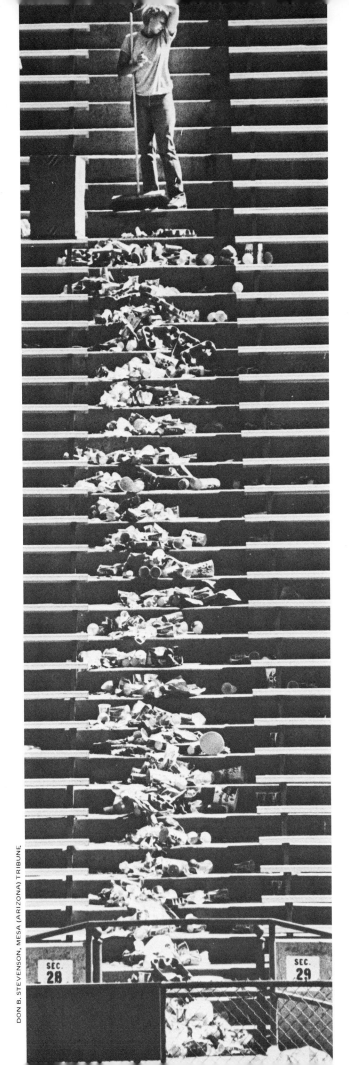

251

LIST OF WINNERS

36th Annual Pictures of the Year Competition

NEWSPAPER PHOTOGRAPHER OF THE YEAR
Christopher Johns, *Topeka Capital-Journal*; Runner-up, Richard Derk, *Chicago Sun-Times*; Third place, John H. White, *Chicago Sun-Times*.

MAGAZINE PHOTOGRAPHER OF THE YEAR
James A. Sugar, *National Geographic*; Runner-up, James Amos, *National Geographic*.

WORLD UNDERSTANDING AWARD
George Wedding, *Palm Beach Post*.

NEWSPAPER DIVISION
SPOT NEWS: First, Hans E. Wendt, *County of San Diego*, "Flight 182 about to crash"; Second, Frank Johnston, *The Washington Post*, "Jonestown destruction"; Third, Norman Y. Lono, *Philadelphia Daily News*, "Arrest of Delbert Africa." Honorable mention: Richard Derk, *Chicago Sun-Times*, "King David church fire."

GENERAL NEWS or DOCUMENTARY: First, Darryl Heikes, *United Press International*, "Successful summit"; Second, Brian Grigsby, *Gainesville Sun*, "Smile at death sentence"; Third, Leo Hetzel, *Long Beach* (California) *Press-Telegram*, "Prostitution bust." Honorable mention: Kent Kobersteen, *Minneapolis Tribune*, "Humphrey farewell"; Frank Johnston, *The Washington Post*, "Longest walk"; Richard Derk, *Chicago Sun-Times*, "Harsh confrontation."

FEATURE PICTURE: First, Greg Dorsett, *Fort Wayne News-Sentinel*, "Close encounters of the 4H kind"; Second, Robert Lachman, *Los Angeles Times*, "The U.S. marines capture a sunbather"; Third, Rick McCarthy, *San Diego Union*, "Trash bird." Honorable mention: William J. Lizdas, *La Crosse* (Wisconsin) *Tribune*, "Right in step"; Gene Puskar, *The As-*

sociated Press/Philadelphia, "Horse auction town"; Norman Y. Lono, *Philadelphia Daily News*, "Somersault."

SPORTS ACTION: First, Ron Kuntz, *United Press International/Cleveland*, "Look out head"; Second, John H. White, *Chicago Sun-Times*, no title (horse race); Third, Melissa Farlow *Courier-Journal and Louisville Times*, "World class crash."

SPORTS FEATURE: First, Jim Jennings, *Virginian Pilot*, "All eyes"; Second, Dave La Belle, *Chanute* (Kansas) *Tribune*, "Cooling Rod Carew's hot bat"; Third, Gary Angell, *United Press International*, "New champ." Honorable mention: Keith Williams, *Courier-Journal and Louisville Times*, "The feel of a champion."

PORTRAIT/PERSONALITY: First, Nick Kelsh, *Columbia* (Missouri) *Daily Tribune*, "Boxer"; Second, Sarah E. Leen, *Arizona Daily Star*, "Yacqui Indian women"; Third, Pat Partington, *Palm Beach Post*, "Bert Lance." Honorable mention: Gary Fong, *San Francisco Chronicle*, "The tax fighter"; Steve Silk, (New Haven) Journal-Courier, "Amazing grace."

PICTORIAL: First, Martha Hartnett, *Chicago Sun-Times*, "Sun dance"; Second, Dick Van Nostrand, *Bay City* (Michigan) *Times*, "Digging out"; Third, Don Bartletti, *San Diego Union*, "Morning paper." Honorable mention: John W. McDonough, *Los Angeles Times/San Diego*, "Grand design"; James Meehan, (New Haven) *Journal-Courier*, "Jawa summit"; Michael Coers, *Courier-Journal and Louisville Times*, "Black and white pasture"; Mark B. Sluder, *Charlotte Observer*, "Chair."

EDITORIAL ILLUSTRATION: First, Tom Herde, *Trenton* (New Jersey) *Times*, "4th of July"; Second, Rob Kinmonth, *Newport News Daily Press-Times Herald*, "Photo for ballet performance"; Third, Duane

Braley, *Minneapolis Star*, "The articulate body." Honorable mention: Joe Elbert, *Miami Herald*, "Last round for E.R.A."; Jim Klepitsch, *Chicago Sun-Times*, "Encroachment on open spaces"; Alan Berner, *Muskegon* (Michigan) *Chronicle*, "TV addicts."

FOOD ILLUSTRATION: First, Fredric Stein, *Chicago Sun-Times*, "Pickling"; Second, Talis Bergmanis, *Gannett Rochester Newspapers*, "Butcher"; Third, Gary S. Chapman, *Fort Meyers News-Press*, "Vegetarian protein." Honorable mention: Dale Guldan, *Milwaukee Journal*, "Coho salmon"; Fredric Stein, *Chicago Sun-Times*, "Strawberries."

FASHION ILLUSTRATION: First, Bob Fila, *Chicago Tribune*, "Beige blouses"; Second, Joe Elbert, *Miami Herald*, "Plastic nails"; Third, Taro Yamasaki, *Detroit Free Press*, "Fall fashion '78."

NEWS PICTURE STORY: First, Frank Johnston, *The Washington Post*, "Jonestown suicide"; Second, Mimi Fuller, *Cincinnati Post*, "Mugging a wino"; Third, Norman Y. Lono, *Philadelphia Daily News*, "Oh my god, they shot a cop." Honorable mention: John H. White, *Chicago Sun-Times*, "Oh god, my babies"; David L. Finch, *Des Moines Register/Tribune*, "Death of a cyclist"; Richard Derk, *Chicago Sun-Times*, "Nazi satisfaction."

FEATURE PICTURE STORY: First, George Wedding, *Palm Beach Post*, "Cancer's undeserving victim"; Second, Nick Kelsh, *Columbia* (Missouri) *Daily Tribune*, "Juvenile deliquents"; Third, Ricardo J. Ferro, *St. Petersburg Times and Evening Independent*, "It gets to be work." Honorable mention: Christopher Johns, *Topeka Capital-Journal*, "Love in a plastic world"; John H. White, *Chicago Sun-Times*, "Champ on wheels."

SPORTS PICTURE STORY: First, Alex Burrows, *Cincinnati Enquirer*, "Senior George Rudd"; Second, John H. White, *Chicago Sun-Times*, "Muhammad Ali training camp"; Third, Andy Hayt, *Los Angeles Times*, "LA mugged by New York tour group." Honorable mention: Karl Kuntz, *The Kentucky Post*, "The kid's first derby"; Christopher Johns, *Topeka Capital-Journal*, "Slip, slidin' away"; Dave Jennings, *Denver Sentinel Newspapers*, "Tying, it's an empty feeling."

MAGAZINE DIVISION

NEWS or DOCUMENTARY: First, James Amos, *National Geographic*, "Space shuttle"; Second, Martin Rogers, *National Geographic*, "Superspill"; Third, Lester Sloan, *Newsweek*, "California fire." Honorable mention: Sam Abell, *National Geographic*, "Sudbury nickel mine"; Lester Millmen, freelance for *Time*, "On the side of the angles"; Martin Rogers, *National Geographic*, "Jaws."

FEATURE PICTURE: First, Dirck Halstead, *Time*, "Jumbo jumble"; Second, Jonathan Blair, *National Geographic*, "Hang in there baby"; Third, David S. Boyer, *National Geographic*, "Log jam." Honorable mention: Dirck Halstead, *Time*, "The gray ghost"; James L. Stanfield, *National Geographic*, "Arab grocer."

SPORTS ACTION: First, David S. Boyer, *National Geographic*, "Inside on the rail"; Second, James A. Sugar, *National Geographic*, "The windsurger"; Third, David S. Boyer, *National Geographic*, "Into the foam." Honorable mention: Sam Abell, *National Geographic*, "Dueling with wind surfers"; Dirck Halstead, *Time*, "Hard right"; Ed Goldfarb, *Black Star*, "New York City Marathon."

SPORTS FEATURE: First, James A. Sugar, *National Geographic*, "Catamaran race"; Second, Bill Weems, *National Geographic*, "Battle prayer."

PORTRAIT/PERSONALITY: First, Sam Abell, *National Geographic*, "Canadian farm boy after harvest"; Second, David Doubilet, *National Geographic*, "Judy Anderson, Miss USA"; Third, James

The judges, left to right: Lee Battaglia, International Communications Agency; Dane Bath, *The New York Times*; Robert Chandler, Bend, Oregon *Bulletin*; Clyde (Red) Hare, freelance, Pittsburgh; Rich Clarkson, *Topeka Capital-Journal*

Amos, *National Geographic*, "WWI drum corp." Honorable mention: Jonathan Blair, *National Geographic*, "American cowboy"; James Amos, *National Geographic*, "George Cavender."

PICTORIAL: First, Nathan Benn, *National Geographic*, "Summer cottages on Atlantic coast"; Second, Sam Abell, *National Geographic*, "Fort George in fog"; Third, Rick Smolan, *Contact Press Images*, "Caravan." Honorable mention: James Sugar, *National Geographic*, "Cormorants at Point Lobos"; James Sugar, *National Geographic*, "Elk in the fog"; Bill Weems, *National Geographic*, "Swamp interlude."

EDITORIAL ILLUSTRATION: First, James Amos, *National Geographic*, "Aluminum in automobiles"; Second, James A. Sugar, *National Geographic*, "Night flight"; Third, Hoag Levins, *Philadelphia Magazine*, "Home from the war." Honorable mention: Dirck Halstead, *Time*, "Kiss and sell."

NEWS or DOCUMENTARY PICTURE STORY: First, Martin Rogers, *National Geographic*, "Breakup of the Amoco Cadiz"; Second, Rick Smolan, *Contact Press Images*, "Alone across the outback."

FEATURE PICTURE STORY: First, Sisse Brimberg, *National Geographic*,

"Apple pickers - migrant worker family"; Second, James Amos, *National Geographic*, "Aluminum wear"; Third, James A. Sugar, *National Geographic*, "California's wild and crazy beaches." Honorable mention: James L. Stanfield, *National Geographic*, "Where Jesus walked"; Jonathan Blair, *National Geographic*, "The outlaw trail."

BEST USE OF PHOTOGRAPHS BY A NEWSPAPER
Columbia (Missouri) *Daily Tribune*. Judges' special recognition: *The Philadelphia Inquirer*.

BEST USE OF PHOTOGRAPHS BY A MAGAZINE
American Photographer.

NEWSPAPER PICTURE EDITOR'S AWARD
Bill Marr, *Columbia* (Missouri) *Daily Tribune*. Judges' special recognition: Brian Lanker, *Eugene* (Oregon) *Register-Guard*.

MAGAZINE PICTURE EDITOR'S AWARD
Sean Callahan and Will Hopkins, *American Photographer*.

NEWSPAPER MAGAZINE PICTURE EDITOR'S AWARD
Maurice Tillman, (Louisville) *Courier-Journal*.

Sam Abell
National Geographic
1145 17th Street, N.W.
Washington, DC 20036
100, 196-197

Thomas J. Abercrombie
National Geographic
1145 17th Street, N.W.
Washington, DC 20036
192-195

Eddie Adams
The Associated Press
143 Linwood Avenue
Bogota, NJ 07603
97

James Amos
National Geographic
1145 17th Street, N.W.
Washington, DC 20036
77

Gary Angell
United Press International
Las Vegas News Bureau
Convention Center
Las Vegas, NV 89109
243

Roger Archibald
Freelance
1423 17th Street
San Francisco, CA 94107
65

Bill Ballenberg
Gloucester County Times
309 S. Broad Street
Woodbury, NJ 08096
212-213

Tony Barnard
Los Angeles Times
Times Mirror Square
Los Angeles, CA 90053
118-119, 122

Don Bartletti
San Diego Union-Tribune
P.O. Box 191
San Diego, CA 92112
165

James L. Bates
Daily World
315 S. Michigan Street
P.O. Box 269
Aberdeen, WA 98520
46

Dick Bell
St. Petersburg Times and
 Evening Independent
P.O. Box 1121
St. Petersburg, FL 33731
132-133

Nathan Benn
National Geographic
1145 17th Street, N.W.
Washington, DC 20036
12-13

Talis Bergmanis
Gannett Rochester
 Newspapers
55 Exchange Street
Rochester, NY 14607
161

Bruce H. Bisping
Minneapolis Tribune
425 Portland Avenue
Minneapolis, MN 55488
149, 208-209, 250

Jonathan Blair
National Geographic
1145 17th Street, N.W.
Washington, DC 20036
98-99

Lori Borgman
Eugene News-Tribune
23 W. 35th Avenue
Eugene, OR 97405
222-223

David S. Boyer
National Geographic
1145 17th Street, N.W.
Washington, DC 20036
23, 232

Duane Braley
Minneapolis Star
425 Portland Avenue
Minneapolis, MN 55488
6

Sisse Brimberg
National Geographic
1145 17th Street, N.W.
Washington, DC 20036
101

Alex Burrows
Cincinnati Enquirer
617 Vine Street
Cincinnati, OH 45202
220-221

Patrick Carroll
New York Daily News
220 E. 42nd Street
New York, NY 10017
50

J. Pat Carter
The Baltimore Sunpapers
501 N. Calvert Street
Baltimore, MD 21203
239

Tim Chapman
Miami Herald
One Herald Plaza
Miami, FL 33101
33

Michael Coers
Courier-Journal and
 Louisville Times
525 West Broadway
Louisville, KY 40202
18-19

Anne Cusack
Chicago Tribune
435 N. Michigan Avenue
Chicago, IL 60611
204-205

Richard Derk
Chicago Sun-Times
401 N. Wabash
Chicago, IL 60611
27, 43, 53, 62, 70, 92-93,
109, 160 (top)

Bob Dickerson
Cincinnati Post
4419 Sullivan Avenue
Cincinnati, OH 45217
104

Michael J. Diemer
Columbia Missourian
University of Missouri
1816 East Broadway, Apt 1-S
Columbia, MO 65201
162

J.G. Domke
The Philadelphia Inquirer
400 North Broad Street
Philadelphia, PA 19101
56-57

Greg Dorsett
The News-Sentinel
600 W. Main
Fort Wayne, IN 46802
139

Steve Dozier
St. Petersburg Times and
 Evening Independent
P.O. Box 1121
St. Petersburg, FL 33731
113

Joe Elbert
Miami Herald
One Herald Plaza
Miami, FL 33101
37, 54-55

Melissa Farlow
Courier-Journal and
 Louisville Times
525 West Broadway
Louisville, KY 40202
3 (top center), 233

Ricardo J. Ferro
St. Petersburg Times and
 Evening Independent
P.O. Box 1121
St. Petersburg, FL 33731
2-3 (top center)

David L. Finch
Des Moines Register and
 Tribune
P.O. Box 957
Des Moines, IA 50304
25

Barry Fitzsimmons
San Diego Union and Tribune
P.O. Box 101
San Diego, CA 92112
10-11

Bryce Flynn
The Providence Journal
75 Fountain Street
Providence, RI 02902
35

Gary E. Fong
San Francisco Chronicle
Fifth and Mission Streets
San Francisco, CA 94119
111

Rich Frishman
The Everett Herald
Everett, WA 98201
52, 202-203

Jim Frost
Chicago Sun-Times
1036 Maple Lane
Elk Grove Village, IL 60007
44, 74-75

Mimi Fuller
Cincinnati Post
501 Garrard Street
Covington, KY 41011
72-73, 206-207

Cramer Gallimore, Jr.
Fayetteville Observer-Times
458 Whitfield Road
Fayetteville, NC 28302
84-85

Erwin Gebhard
Newspapers Inc.
(Milwaukee Journal and
 Sentinel)
333 West State Street
Milwaukee, WI 53201
24

Raymond K. Gehman
Columbia Missourian
University of Missouri
Columbia, MO 65201
3 (bottom left)

Gianni Giansanti
The Associated Press
50 Rockfeller Plaza
New York, NY 10020
34

Ed Goldfarb
Black Star
450 Park Avenue South
New York, NY 10016
224

Bernard Gotfryd
Newsweek
444 Madison Avenue
New York, NY 10022
102

Arthur Grace
Sygma
3246 N Street, N.W.
Washington, DC 20007
106-107

Keith Graham
Columbia Missourian and
 Miami Herald
821 E. Walnut, Apt. 200
Columbia, MO 65201
152-153

Bryan K. Grigsby
Springfield Newspapers, Inc.
651 Boonville
Springfield, MO 65801
68, 246-247

Dirck Halstead
Time
Room 2850
Time Life Building
New York, NY 10020
17

Jeffrey Hamilton
Yakima Herald-Republic
114 N. 4th Street
Yakima, WA 98908
148

Martha Harnett
Los Angeles Times
Times Mirror Square
Los Angeles, CA 90053
158-159

Jebb A. Harris
Courier-Journal and
   Louisville Times
525 West Broadway
Louisville, KY 40202
(half title page), 157

David Hausam
Freelance
University of Missouri
1701 S. Beacon
Sedalia, MO 65301
20

Andy Hayt
Los Angeles Times
Times Mirror Square
Los Angeles, CA 90053
234-235

Darryl Heikes
United Press International
901 Lakeside Avenue
Cleveland, OH 44114
40-41

Diana Mara Henry
Freelance
1160 Fifth Avenue
New York, NY 10029
45

Tom Herde
Trenton Times
500 Perry Street
Trenton, NJ 08605
6

Leo Hetzel
Long Beach Press-Telegram
604 Pine Avenue
Long Beach, CA 90801
69

Donald Hornstein
Freelance
506 Clinkscales
Columbia, MO 65201
122 (top)

Deris A. Jeannette
Los Angeles Times
1375 Sunflower
Costa Mesa, CA 92626
116

Jim Jennings
The Virginian Pilot/Ledger
   Star
150 W. Brambleton Avenue
Norfolk, VA 23510
231

Christopher G. Johns
Topeka Capital-Journal
616 Jefferson Street
Topeka, KA 66607
71, 229

Curtis Johnson
Independent Press-Telegram
604 Pine Avenue
Long Beach, CA 90801
117

Frank B. Johnston
The Washington Post
1150 15th Street, N.W.
Washington, DC 20071
29, 30-31, 32, 62

Tom Kasser
San Bernardino Sun
399 N. "D" Street
San Bernardino, CA 92401
2 (bottom left)

Nick Kelsh
Columbia Daily Tribune
1608 Wilson Avenue
Columbia, MO 65201
(contents page), 135, 136-137

Tom Kennedy
Gainesville Sun
P.O. Drawer A
Gainesville, FL 32602
223

Mitch Kezar
Tampa Tribune
202 S. Parker Street
Tampa, FL 33602
138

Rob Kinmonth
Newport News Daily Press-
   Times Herald
Newport News, VA 23601
7

Kent Kobersteen
Minneapolis Tribune
425 Portland Avenue
Minneapolis, MN 55488
66-67, 141

Ron Kuner
Akron Beacon Journal
44 E. Exchange Street
Akron, OH 44328
210-211

Ron Kuntz
United Press International
901 Lakeside Avenue
Cleveland, OH 44114
242 (top)

Dave La Belle
The Chanute Tribune
15 N. Evergreen
Chanute, KA 66720
244

Robert Lachman
Los Angeles Times
225 Broadway, No. 820
San Diego, CA 92101
94-95

Len Lahman
Los Angeles Times
San Diego County Edition
Central Federal Tower
Suite 820
San Diego, CA 92101
47

Brian Lanker
Eugene Register-Guard
975 High Street
Eugene, OR 97401
130-131

Rex D. Larsen
The Grand Rapids Press
960 Parmelee N.W.
Grand Rapids, MI 49504
248-249

Sarah E. Leen
Arizona Daily Star
1907A Gordon Street
Columbia, MO 65201
124-125, 128

William J. Lizdas
LaCrosse Tribune
401 North 3rd Street
La Crosse, WI 54601
156-157

Jerry Lodriguss
Times-Picayune
1800 Giuffrias
Metairie, LA 70001
215, 243

Norman Y. Lono
Philadelphia Daily News
400 North Broad Street
Philadelphia, PA 19101
56-59, 105

Phil Mascione
Chicago Tribune
435 N. Michigan Avenue
Chicago, IL 60611
218-219

R. Norman Matheny
The Christian Science
   Monitor
910 Sixteenth Street
Washington, DC 20006
107

Ed McCain
Columbia Missourian
University of Missouri
Columbia, MO 65201
122

John W. McDonough
Los Angeles Times
San Diego County Edition
225 Broadway, Suite 820
San Diego, CA 92101
26, 60-61

James Meehan
The Journal-Courier
367 Orange Street
New Haven, CT 06511
236-237

William Meyer
Milwaukee Journal
333 W. State Street
Milwaukee, WI 53202
129

Peter Monsees
The Record
150 River Street
Hackensack, NJ 07601
3 (bottom right)

John Moran
The Miami News
One Herald Plaza
Miami, FL 33101
48-49

Robert A. Nandell
Des Moines Register
715 Locust Street
Des Moines, IA 50304
51

Michael O'Brien
The Miami News
One Herald Plaza
Miami, FL 33101
89

Pat Partington
Palm Beach Post
2751 S. Dixie Highway
West Palm Beach, FL 33405
111, 160 (bottom)

Mark Perlstein
Dallas Times Herald
1101 Pacific Avenue
Dallas, TX 75202
39

David Peterson
Des Moines Register
715 Locust Street
Des Moines, IA 50304
3 (top right), 238

Skip Peterson
Dayton Daily News
Fourth and Luddow Street
Dayton, OH 45401
140

Gene J. Puskar
The Associated Press/
   Philadelphia
Box 7784
Philadelphia, PA 19101
146-147

Kenneth R. Randolph
The Journal-Courier
29 Artizan Street
New Haven, CT 06511
108

Larry Reese
Dallas Morning News
Communications Center
Dallas, TX 75265
22